THE PSYCHOLOGY OF CONSPIRACY THEORIES

Who believes in conspiracy theories, and why are some people more susceptible to them than others? What are the consequences of such beliefs? Has a conspiracy theory ever turned out to be true?

The Psychology of Conspiracy Theories debunks the myth that conspiracy theories are a modern phenomenon, exploring their broad social contexts, from politics to the workplace. The book explains why some people are more susceptible to these beliefs than others, and how they are produced by recognizable and predictable psychological processes.

Featuring examples such as the 9/11 terrorist attacks and climate change, *The Psychology of Conspiracy Theories* shows us that while such beliefs are not always irrational and are not a pathological trait, they can be harmful to individuals and society.

Jan-Willem van Prooijen is an Associate Professor of Social and Organizational Psychology at VU Amsterdam, and Senior Researcher at the Netherlands Institute for the Study of Crime and Law Enforcement.

THE PSYCHOLOGY OF EVERYTHING

The Psychology of Everything is a series of books which debunk the myths and pseudo-science surrounding some of life's biggest questions.

The series explores the hidden psychological factors that drive us, from our sub-conscious desires and aversions, to the innate social instincts handed to us across the generations. Accessible, informative, and always intriguing, each book is written by an expert in the field, examining how research-based knowledge compares with popular wisdom, and illustrating the potential of psychology to enrich our understanding of humanity and modern life.

Applying a psychological lens to an array of topics and contemporary concerns – from sex to addiction to conspiracy theories – The Psychology of Everything will make you look at everything in a new way.

Titles in the series:

For further information about this series please visit www.thepsychologyofeverything.co.uk

THE PSYCHOLOGY OF CONSPIRACY THEORIES

JAN-WILLEM VAN PROOIJEN

LONDON AND NEW YORK

First published 2018
by Routledge
2 Park Square, Milton Park, Abingdon, Oxon OX14 4RN

and by Routledge
711 Third Avenue, New York, NY 10017

Routledge is an imprint of the Taylor & Francis Group, an informa business

© 2018 Jan-Willem van Prooijen

The right of Jan-Willem van Prooijen to be identified as author of this work has been asserted by him in accordance with sections 77 and 78 of the Copyright, Designs and Patents Act 1988.

British Library Cataloguing-in-Publication Data
A catalogue record for this book is available from the British Library

Library of Congress Cataloging-in-Publication Data
Names: Prooijen, Jan-Willem van, 1975– author.
Title: Psychology of conspiracy theories / Jan-Willem van Prooijen.
Description: New York, NY : Routledge, 2018. | Includes
    bibliographical references.
Identifiers: LCCN 2017040641 (print) | LCCN 2017052772 (ebook) |
    ISBN 9781315525419 (Master e-book) | ISBN 9781138696099
    (hardback) | ISBN 9781138696105 (pbk.) |
    ISBN 9781315436012 (ebk)
Subjects: LCSH: Conspiracy theories.
Classification: LCC HV6275 (ebook) | LCC HV6275 .P756 2018 (print) |
    DDC 001.9—dc23
LC record available at https://lccn.loc.gov/2017040641

ISBN: 978-1-138-69609-9 (hbk)
ISBN: 978-1-138-69610-5 (pbk)
ISBN: 978-1-315-52541-9 (ebk)

Typeset in Joanna
by Apex CoVantage, LLC

CONTENTS

PREFACE

Climate change is a hoax perpetrated by the Chinese. The pharma-ceutical industry hides evidence that vaccines cause autism. And there is a major conspiracy to cover up the fact that Barack Obama was born in Kenya. These are conspiracy theories that were propagated during the 2016 presidential campaign of Donald Trump. Scientists, journalists, policy makers, and other critics portray these theories as naïve, far-fetched, not supported by evidence, or simply ridiculous. But why then do so many people believe such conspiracy theories? The appeal of these conspiracy theories among voters was substan-tial enough for Trump to win the Electoral College and become the 45th US president. This suggests that conspiracy theories cannot be dismissed as harmless entertainment or as manifestations of mental illness. Conspiracy theories are common among regular citizens and determine real and impactful choices in life such as who to vote for, whether to get one's child vaccinated, whether to place effort into reducing one's carbon footprint, whether to use contraceptives, and whether to aggress against dissimilar outgroups. It is time for the social sciences to take the widespread societal phenomenon of con-spiracy theories seriously.

Who believes conspiracy theories, and who disbelieves them? Under what circumstances are people particularly susceptible to conspiracy theories? What are the consequences of believing in conspiracy theories? And what can policy makers do to reduce belief in conspiracy theories? These important questions are the domain of psychology. The present book was designed to provide a short, accessible, and state-of-the-art overview of the psychology of conspiracy theories. The main thesis of this book is that – contrary to views that explain conspiracy theories through pathology – belief in conspiracy theories is widespread among many citizens because they are rooted in normal psychological processes. Conspiracy theories originate through the same cognitive processes that produce other types of belief (e.g., new age, spirituality), they reflect a desire to protect one's own group against a potentially hostile outgroup, and they are often grounded in strong ideologies. Conspiracy theories are a natural defensive reaction to feelings of uncertainty and fear, blaming dissimilar outgroups for the distressing circumstances that one has to deal with.

Although this is a short book, there are more people to thank than space allows. At Routledge I thank Ceri Griffiths for embarking with me on this project and Elizabeth Rankin for her help. I also thank Michael Strang, who brought the new Routledge "Psychology of . . ." series to my attention and persuaded me to write this book.

I greatly appreciate the many collaborations I have with scholars and students around the world on the psychology of conspiracy theories, and many of the ideas described in this book originated through discussions or joint research with them. I would like to particularly mention Paul van Lange, André Krouwel, Karen Douglas, Nils Jostmann, Reinout de Vries, Mark van Vugt, Robbie Sutton, Roland Imhoff, Michele Acker, Eric van Dijk, Thomas Pollet, Clara de Inocencio, and Olivier Klein. I also thank the many scholars that I met (and currently collaborate with on the topic of conspiracy theories) through two COST Action networks that I am privileged to be part of: COST Action "Social psychological dynamics of historical representations in the enlarged European Union" and COST Action "Comparative analysis of conspiracy theories".

In my personal life I would like to thank John Ensberg, who believes far more conspiracy theories than I do yet also is one of my best friends. Finally, I thank my wife, Claudia van Prooijen-van Remundt: Somehow she manages to increase my productivity by frequently distracting me. Thanks to her for creating some balance, and I am glad to find out every day that there really is more to life than science.

Jan-Willem van Prooijen
Amsterdam, 26 July 2017

1

PSYCHOLOGY OF CONSPIRACY THEORIES

The 9/11 terrorist strikes are not only among the most impactful events in modern history but also among the best-documented ones. Professional news crews and New York City residents made live video recordings as this terrible event unfolded, which were widely broadcasted. We all have seen the footage of United Airlines Flight 175 crashing in the South Tower of the World Trade Center from any possible angle and were able to see how these impressive buildings collapsed like a house of cards. But although the footage is objectively the same, people appear to differ widely in what they are seeing in these recordings. Many people see how a passenger plane that was hijacked by suicide terrorists exploded upon collision, ultimately causing the destruction of the Twin Towers. Many other people, however, see direct evidence for controlled demolition: Not suicide terrorist but the US government was responsible for the plane crash, and not the impact of the plane but explosives that were hidden within the buildings caused the destruction of the Twin Towers.

The allegations that the US government helped to cause 9/11 are reflected in conspiracy theories that one can easily find on Internet and social media. Large groups of concerned citizens – such as the "9/11-for-truth" movement – made documentaries, published books and articles, and organized rallies to convince the public that the US government is withholding the truth about these events. Furthermore, there are many different variants of 9/11 conspiracy theories. The relatively "milder" variants propose that the US government is merely an accessory, and for instance assume that public officials knew that the terrorist strikes were coming yet deliberately failed to prevent them. Other variants make allegations of a more active role for the US government and propose that public officials directly organized and carried out these attacks. These latter conspiracy theories often portray the 9/11 strikes as a "false-flag operation" – an attack that was designed to look as if it were carried out by other countries or organizations in order to justify far-reaching actions such as war. These false-flag 9/11 conspiracy theories are well known for claims such as that the airplanes were remote-controlled, that explosives caused the destruction of the Twin Towers, that the Pentagon was hit by a rocket instead of a passenger plane, and so on.

Whether we believe in them or not, such conspiracy theories surely are fascinating. Conspiracy theories appeal to a basic, dark fear that we all are string puppets under the control of powerful, sinister, and invisible forces. Conspiracy theories refer to hidden, secret, and malignant organizations that influence our lives without us being aware of it. Many conspiracy theories elicit a sense of "What if?" among people: Can these theories be true, and what would that imply for how we live our lives? Do we really understand the way that the world operates, or have we been deceived all along? There is something irresistibly mysterious, intriguing, but also frightening to a credible conspiracy theory, and therefore conspiracy theories have the potential to capture the attention of a broad audience.

Such widespread appeal can for instance be seen in the prominent place that conspiracy theories have in popular culture. Many well-known blockbuster movies are based on the central idea of people being deceived or threatened by a conspiracy of evil and hidden forces. In *The Truman Show*, the lead character played by Jim Carrey is unaware that his whole life actually is a popular reality show under the control of a TV station. Everyone he knows – his friends, his family, and even his wife – are part of the conspiracy designed to trick him into believing that he leads a normal life. Another example, which seems very different but is actually based on the same conspiratorial principle, is *The Matrix* – a movie in which viewers are led to believe that life as we know it is a virtual reality illusion that has been deliberately pulled over our eyes. Human beings actually are prisoners of a conspiracy of hostile and highly intelligent computers, who utilize our life energy as efficient batteries.

What connects *The Truman Show* and *The Matrix* is that they portray rather existential conspiracy theories, implying that our life in its most minor details can be controlled by a conspiracy without our knowledge. But there are also many movies that are based on more common conspiracy theories, depicting how government agencies or other organizations use excessive power to persecute citizens. Often these conspiracies have highly advanced technology at their disposal, which enables them to effectively track down their victims (e.g., *Eagle Eye*, *The Net*, *Enemy of the State*). Personally I am a big fan of the Netflix original series *House of Cards*, which describes how a corrupt politician makes a career (all the way to becoming US president) through lies, deception, bribery, intimidation, coercion, and even murder. These movies and series all share a key element of many conspiracy theories, which is a depiction of powerful people or institutions as evilminded, dangerous, and largely operating in the shadows.

One factor that contributes to the widespread appeal of conspiracy theories is the possibility that they might actually be true – and in fact, conspiracies sometimes can and do occur. An infamous example of a real conspiracy at the highest political level is the "Iran-Contra affair", which took place during the 1980s. US government officials were found to have secretly facilitated the sale of weapons to Iran (even though Iran was subject to an arms embargo) and then used the profits to secretly fund the Contra Rebels in Nicaragua (even though further funding of the Contras had been explicitly prohibited by Congress). Another real conspiracy was the so-called Tuskegee-syphilis experiment, in which scientists pretended to offer free health care to African-American men. In reality, they studied the natural development of untreated syphilis, involving 399 men who had syphilis but were unaware of their condition and 201 healthy men as a control group. The experiment lasted for 40 years (1932 to 1972). During this time, these men were never informed that they were taking part in an experiment, nor were they informed about their actual medical condition, and their illness was left untreated. As a result, many men suffered the consequences of untreated syphilis, including death.

The Holocaust also was the result of a real conspiracy. While Jews were already widely persecuted and killed in Nazi Germany in the 1930s and early 1940s, initially the Nazis had hoped that due to the hostile climate most Jews would leave the country voluntarily. This did not happen on the scale desired by Hitler, however, and in January 1942 a conspiracy of 15 high-ranked Nazis and SS-officers secretly gathered in a villa at Wannsee near Berlin. Although Hitler did not attend in person, the meeting had the purpose of designing a concrete plan to carry out Hitler's recent orders – which boiled down to "physically exterminating" all of the Jews in Europe. This meeting, commonly known as the "Wannsee conference", marked the beginning of the mass deportation of Jews to Nazi death camps, where they were murdered in gas chambers on an unprecedented scale. The Holocaust is now recognized as one of the biggest tragedies in human history. Yet it was not until 1947 that a legal prosecutor found evidence that the Wannsee conference actually took place, by discovering the strictly classified minutes of this secret meeting.

This book is about the psychology of conspiracy theories. There are many different conspiracy theories that circle the Internet, some of them plausible or at least theoretically possible (e.g., perhaps secret service agencies sometimes do push the limits of what is legally or morally acceptable, as the Snowden revelations suggest), others are rather outlandish and highly unlikely to be true (e.g., the conspiracy theory that the earth is ruled by a race of alien lizards disguised as humans). Furthermore, there are many examples of actual conspiracy formation throughout history – ranging from modern times (Angela Merkel's mobile phone really was tapped by the US secret service) to for instance the Roman Senate conspiracy that killed Julius Caesar – and hence, not all conspiracy theories are necessarily irrational. Despite all the differences among the conspiracy theories that people endorse, in the present book I will argue that people's tendency to believe in conspiracy theories is rooted in similar, recognizable, and predictable psychological processes.

WHAT IS A CONSPIRACY THEORY?

Although various definitions of conspiracy theories exist, the one that I favor is "the belief that a number of actors join together in secret agreement, in order to achieve a hidden goal which is perceived to be unlawful or malevolent".[1] This is a broad definition, and accordingly, conspiracy theories can take many forms and emerge in many different spheres of life. People can hold conspiracy theories about the government, or governmental institutions (e.g., secret service agencies). People can hold conspiracy theories about entire branches of industry (e.g., the pharmaceutical industry) or about scientific research (e.g., climate change conspiracy theories). Employees on the work floor also often hold conspiracy beliefs about their management, such as beliefs that managers have a hidden agenda to pursue selfish goals. Conspiracy theories may occur in sports (e.g., beliefs that the referee was bribed by the opposing team). Also in their personal life, people may hold conspiracy theories by thinking that others conspire against them personally – although the latter, more personally oriented forms of conspiracy theories are in scientific discourse regarded as examples of "paranoia" and are qualitatively different from conspiracy beliefs that make assumptions of how large groups of citizens are being deceived by formal authorities.

To specify the definition of conspiracy theories further, I propose that any belief needs to possess at least five critical ingredients in order to qualify as a conspiracy theory. They are:

1 *Patterns* – Any conspiracy theory explains events by establishing nonrandom connections between actions, objects, and people. Put differently, a conspiracy theory assumes that the chain of

incidents that caused a suspect event did not occur through coincidence.

2 *Agency* – A conspiracy theory assumes that a suspect event was caused on purpose by intelligent actors: There was a sophisticated and detailed plan that was intentionally developed and carried out.

3 *Coalitions* – A conspiracy theory always involves a coalition or group of multiple actors, usually but not necessarily humans (examples of nonhuman conspiracy theories are *The Matrix* and the "alien lizard" conspiracy theories). If one believes that a single individual, a lone wolf, is responsible for a suspect event, this belief is not a conspiracy theory – for the simple reason that it does not involve a conspiracy.

4 *Hostility* – A conspiracy theory tends to assume the suspected coalition to pursue goals that are evil, selfish, or otherwise not in the public interest. Certainly people may sometimes suspect a benevolent conspiracy, and benevolent conspiracies indeed do exist (as adults we conspire every year to convince children of the existence of Santa Claus). But in the present book, as well as in other literature on this topic, the term "conspiracy theory" is exclusive to conspiracies that are suspected to be hostile. Belief in benevolent conspiracy theories is likely to be grounded in different psychological processes than described in this book.

5 *Continued secrecy* – Conspiracy theories are about coalitions that operate in secret. With "continued" secrecy, I mean that the conspiracy has not yet been exposed by hard evidence, and hence its assumed operations remain secret and uncertain. A conspiracy that is exposed and hence proven true (e.g., the Wannsee conference) is no longer a "theory"; instead, it is an established example of actual conspiracy formation. Conspiracy theories are thus by definition unproven.

These five qualities distinguish belief in conspiracy theories from many other beliefs that people may hold. Take, for instance, the common supernatural belief that it is possible to get into contact with the souls of deceased relatives. Such belief in the existence of ghosts shares at least two and arguably three of the key ingredients of conspiracy beliefs, but not all five of them. Belief in ghosts involves patterns (i.e., it makes assumptions of how life after death develops in a nonrandom fashion; furthermore, believing in ghosts is likely to influence how one causally explains mysterious events in life) and it also involves agency (i.e., the ghosts are typically assumed to have goals, emotions, and desires, and they are for instance capable of communicating with living people through a medium). Belief in ghosts does not require "continued secrecy", but one might say that there are at least parallels with this ingredient, as ghost beliefs are also unproven, pertain to invisible forces, and are characterized by mystery. But the coalition and hostility elements are lacking, at least as necessary requirements for this belief. Ghosts may be considered to be hostile, but they do not necessarily need to be in order to believe in them. Furthermore, one does not need to make the additional assumption that groups of ghosts organize meetings to design plans of how to harm people. A core aspect of conspiracy beliefs that makes them unique as compared to other forms of belief is that such beliefs involve a secret and hostile group of actors.

PSYCHOLOGY OF CONSPIRACY THEORIES

"Have you ever considered the possibility that our theories might be true?" This is a question that I regularly get through email from Dutch citizens who are active on conspiracy websites. Often these messages have an angry tone, voiced by citizens who somehow feel offended by my research on conspiracy theories and who seem keen on persuading me that Ebola really was created in the lab, or that 9/11 really was an inside job. These messages typically (and wrongly) assume that if one studies the psychology of conspiracy theories, one necessarily proposes that all the conspiracy theories that people believe are invalid, or that people who believe in conspiracy theories are pathological. I have two responses to these email senders. The first is that, next time, they might wish to read the work of an academic more carefully before sending such an angry email – if they would have done so, they would have found out that besides conspiracy theories I also do research (and recently published a book) on the human tendency towards cheating and corruption, which includes the question why people sometimes actually conspire to pursue selfish ends.[2] It is well known that corruption – and hence, actual conspiracy formation – is common, and I do not know of a single scientist who argues otherwise.

But second, and more importantly, the psychology of conspiracy theories is not a question of which conspiracy theories are true or false – it is a question of who does or does not believe in them. There are many conspiracy theories that can be considered irrational in the face of logic or scientific evidence, and the fact that many people nevertheless believe in them is good reason to study this topic (more about that later). Furthermore, I am willing to submit here that I am highly skeptical of some of the rather grandiose conspiracy theories that circle the Internet. I find it highly implausible that Ebola was created in the lab. Furthermore, I firmly believe that 9/11 was carried out by a group of 19 Al Qaeda suicide terrorists – and this is not a conspiracy theory by the given definition, because the evidence to support this claim is so overwhelming that it is safe to say that the conspiracy of these 19 terrorists has been exposed (i.e., there is no "continued secrecy"). Finally, while I consider it possible that Lee Harvey Oswald received help from unknown others while preparing to assassinate JFK (and hence that there may have been a conspiracy), I consider it unlikely that this help came from the CIA, the Russians, or the Cubans. But what I think about these conspiracy theories is not the focus of this book.

This book focuses on the *psychology* of conspiracy theories, which is the scientific study of why some people are more likely than others to believe in conspiracy theories. Typical questions that are part of the psychology of conspiracy theories are: What personality factors determine whether someone believes or disbelieves conspiracy theories? To what extent does belief in one conspiracy theory (e.g., about the pharmaceutical industry) predict the likelihood of believing in a different conspiracy theory (e.g., JFK)? In what situations are people more and in what situations are people less likely to believe in conspiracy theories? And what are the consequences of conspiracy theories for believers' feelings and behaviors? To study these issues, one does not need the conspiracy theory that is under investigation to be necessarily false, nor does newly emerging evidence that an actual conspiracy occurred compromise any of the conclusions that are drawn in this research area.

Let me briefly illuminate this principle by drawing a comparison with the psychology of religion. Many social scientists study religious beliefs, and one typical finding in this research domain is that religious people cling more strongly to their faith in unpredictable, frightening situations. (I'm sure many readers recognize the desire to say a little prayer when they are scared.) The theory behind this finding is that people have a need to feel that they are to some extent in control of their environment. Unpredictable situations make people feel less in control, and as a consequence, people start relying more strongly on external sources of control – such as God.[3] Is it necessary for this line of research to also prove or disprove – or at least make assumptions of – the actual existence of God? My answer would be a succinct "No": The mere observation that people differ strongly in their religiousness is sufficient to raise the legitimate question why some people do, and others do not, entertain certain religious beliefs. The finding that people are more religious in frightening situations teaches us something about the psychological processes underlying religion. For instance, one possible interpretation of these research findings is that belief in God can be a source of comfort in scary situations. This conclusion does not make any judgment of the question whether God actually exists or not, nor does it imply a value judgment for believers or nonbelievers.

The principle for the psychology of conspiracy theories is the same: It is perfectly possible to study these beliefs without knowing for sure whether certain specific conspiracy theories are true or false. As a matter of fact, I know of one published research study that examined belief in a conspiracy theory that later on did turn out to be true. The study focused specifically on the Watergate affair. In 1972, a group of five men were caught burglarizing the Democratic National Committee headquarters in the Watergate hotel, Washington, DC. The burglary was part of a bigger scheme that involved influential Republicans spying on the Democratic Party for political gain, which included bugging the offices of Democratic opponents and other abuses of power. Many high-ranking White House officials, including President Nixon himself, initially denied any involvement after the burglars were caught. In the investigation that followed, however, the evidence increasingly suggested that Nixon actively tried to cover up his personal involvement in the burglary and other illegal activities associated with it. Eventually, the public release of tape recordings that Nixon had of meetings held in his office supported his role in a cover-up, leading him to resign his presidency on 9 August 1974.

Two academic researchers, Thomas Wright and Jack Arbuthnot, conducted a study on how suspicious people were of the Watergate affair as it unfolded.[4] The study was conducted in May 1973 – which was before the Senate hearings had taken place, before the Supreme Court had ordered Nixon's tape recordings to be made public, and hence before the personal involvement of Nixon in the Watergate affair was proven beyond reasonable doubt. At that point in time, the allegation that President Nixon himself was an active player in the Watergate scandal was still a "conspiracy theory" according to all the five ingredients presented earlier. In their study, the researchers were particularly interested in the factors that would predict how suspicious people were of the possible role that Nixon might have played during Watergate. They focused on interpersonal trust and tested if people who have a structural tendency to distrust others would be more suspicious of Nixon's involvement. They also examined the role of political ideology and tested whether Democrats or Republicans would be more suspicious of Nixon. The results indicated that the stronger people distrust others in their daily life, the more likely they were to perceive a conspiracy involving Nixon. Also, Democrats were more likely than Republicans to believe this conspiracy theory.

What followed is well known: Yes, it was true. Nixon actively tried to cover up his role in Watergate and was personally involved in the illegal extraction of sensitive information about his political opponents, which he used to his political advantage. Nixon's personal involvement in the Watergate scandal no longer classifies as a "conspiracy theory", given that there is no continued secrecy anymore: The conspiracy has been exposed, it is therefore no longer a "theory", and Watergate has become a textbook example of an actual conspiracy that took place at the highest political level. Should we now abandon Wright and Arbuthnot's conclusions? Does the fact that this conspiracy theory turned out true compromise their results in any way?

I do not think so. While few people dispute the role of Nixon in Watergate nowadays, back in May 1973 this issue was still unproven and subject to intense public debate. The research question of Wright and Arbuthnot was not whether this particular conspiracy theory was true or false; the question was what personality and political factors would predict citizens' belief in it at a point in time when the evidence for this theory was still inconclusive. The results that they observed have been replicated by multiple researchers and in the context of many other conspiracy theories. People who are inclined to distrust other people are more likely to believe in conspiracy theories than people who are inclined to trust other people. Furthermore, people particularly believe in conspiracy theories about groups that are ideologically dissimilar. Democrats therefore are more likely to believe theories that involve a Republican conspiracy, and Republicans are more likely to believe theories that involve a Democrat conspiracy. These were the conclusions that followed from Wright and Arbuthnot's study, and these conclusions still hold today.

The psychology of conspiracy theories examines who believes or disbelieves these theories instead of whether a certain conspiracy theory is true or false. I have no more knowledge about the likelihood of certain conspiracy theories than other citizens, nor do I have access to classified government intelligence – and this is not necessary to study the psychology of conspiracy theories. In the chapters that follow, I will highlight situational and personality factors that predict how susceptible people are to conspiracy theories. In the remainder of this chapter, however, I will deal with two lingering issues regarding the psychology of conspiracy theories: Should we care about whether or not people hold such beliefs, and should we pathologize people who believe in conspiracy theories – including the relatively absurd ones?

SHOULD WE CARE ABOUT CONSPIRACY THEORIES?

Psychology offers a scientific approach that helps to objectively establish what personality or situational factors determine belief or disbelief in conspiracy theories. Now that we have established that this approach implies that we are not trying to prove or disprove a particular conspiracy theory, an important question becomes whether we should care about conspiracy beliefs at all. If some conspiracy theories can be true, is it not desirable that groups of citizens investigate them? Should we consider conspiracy theories as a form of harmless entertainment? Or can conspiracy theories actually be detrimental to people's lives and to society at large, and should we be concerned about those beliefs?

My argument is the latter: We should be concerned, because in many cases conspiracy theories are irrational, yet they can do real harm to real people. Let me first establish that I am not saying that we should follow the leaders of our society – politicians, managers, powerful media figures – without any criticism or scrutiny. A healthy critical mind-set implies that we should carefully evaluate the actions of those in power and express concern if we see bad policy or suspect malpractice. Admittedly, sometimes there can be a thin line between healthy skepticism versus destructive conspiracy theorizing. But a critical mindset does not mean uncritically accepting any bizarre or far-fetched conspiracy theory. While one can surely find examples of actual conspiracy formation, the truth is that the vast majority of conspiracy theories that citizens have endorsed throughout the ages turned out to be false.[5] My concern is particularly targeted at the many conspiracy theories that defy logic, ignore scientific evidence, or place blame on innocent people or groups – and in many ways belief in such conspiracy theories can be damaging. What people believe drives their behavior; and the more irrational these beliefs are, the more irrational the behavior it produces.

At present the Internet is filled with misinformation about vaccines, making many people reluctant to get themselves or their children vaccinated. A lot of this misinformation is rooted in conspiracy theories. One pertinent idea that many people within the anti-vaccine movement have is that vaccines cause autism and that the pharmaceutical industry conspires to keep the evidence for this a secret. As a result, many people avoid vaccines, putting themselves, their children, and others at unnecessary risk for dangerous and avoidable illnesses. Scientific evidence shows no relationship whatsoever between vaccines and autism. The discovery of vaccines has been a major medical breakthrough that protects citizens from life-threatening illnesses, and we all have reason to be grateful for this important scientific accomplishment. Any responsible parents should make sure that their children get the appropriate vaccines at the right time. It is belief in conspiracy theories that makes many parents decide otherwise.

Conspiracy beliefs also influence voting behavior and can therefore determine the outcomes of elections that shape society. In Chapter 5 I will illuminate that belief in conspiracy theories is associated with a preference for relatively extreme political currents: radical socialist parties at the left end of the political spectrum and anti-immigration parties at the right end of the political spectrum. Donald Trump became US president in the highly polarized 2016 US presidential election, and I find it stunning how he managed to gather massive support – enough for him to win the electoral college – by spreading irrational conspiracy theories such as that climate change is a hoax perpetrated by the Chinese or that there is a conspiracy to hide evidence that Obama was not born in the US. What people believe determines their behavior; and if a political candidate propagates conspiracy theories that many people find appealing and plausible, voting for that candidate becomes a viable option.

Conspiracy theories can sometimes determine the most impactful choices at the highest political level. In 2002, former President

George W. Bush literally said, "Right now, Iraq is expanding and improving facilities that were used for the production of biological weapons." Another, comparable quote (from 2003) was: "Intelligence gathered by this and other governments leaves no doubt that the Iraq regime continues to possess and conceal some of the most lethal weapons ever devised." Compare these quotes with the five key ingredients of conspiracy theories: There are patterns (there is a threat and Iraq is causing it), agency (Iraq is doing this on purpose), a coalition (the Saddam Hussein administration), hostility (Iraq is not developing these weapons out of friendship), and continued secrecy (Iraq is concealing these weapons, and we have in fact never seen them). The belief that Iraq was hiding weapons of mass destruction fits any definition of conspiracy theories that I am aware of – and as history has taught us, it was a false belief. The uncomfortable conclusion is that the national and international support that Bush gathered to go to war against Iraq was based on an invalid conspiracy theory. This is by no means an anomaly: Historians have noted that most, if not all, wars that were fought in the past few centuries involved widespread conspiracy theories about the enemy group at both sides of the conflict.[6]

Conspiracy theories often are not a harmless pastime. They can be damaging to people's health, they can stimulate aggression towards other people or groups, they can undermine necessary efforts to solve the real problems that pose a threat to our existence (e.g., climate change conspiracy theories), they determine what political leaders citizens vote for, and so on. There can be beneficial effects of conspiracy theories as well, sometimes: Conspiracy theories can improve transparency of leaders and open up a debate within society about important topics. But most of the effects of conspiracy theories are harmful: for believers, for their social environment, and for society. This suggests good reason to study these beliefs: Understanding the psychological roots of conspiracy theories might ultimately help in finding ways to make citizens more critically examine them – which is important for conspiracy theories that are highly unlikely to be true.

IS BELIEF IN CONSPIRACY THEORIES PATHOLOGICAL?

Passenger airplane engines often leave a condensation trail. These cloud-like trails in the sky are caused by water particles in the exhaust gases, which are quickly transformed into ice crystals due to low temperatures at high altitudes. But so-called "chemtrail" conspiracy theories assume an evil scheme behind these condensation trails. According to chemtrail conspiracy theories, airplane condensation trails are actually chemical or biological substances that an evil conspiracy – usually the government – sprays over the population in order to influence their behavior. For instance, one common variant of the theory is that these chemicals keep the population meek and docile, thereby allowing the government to carry out its evil plans without having to fear for a revolution by a righteously outraged crowd.

It is safe to say that this conspiracy theory is irrational. If passenger planes would indeed be equipped with technology to spray chemicals, airline technicians doing a routine check-up on a plane would easily discover this. Furthermore, scientific measurements would quickly detect the presence of strange, unknown, or harmful chemicals in the atmosphere and would also be able to track down where these chemicals come from. None of this has happened. Should we consider belief in this irrational conspiracy theory as pathological? Certainly it might be tempting to dismiss chemtrail believers as mentally ill. But the evidence suggests otherwise. Or, let me put it this way: If belief in such a relatively absurd conspiracy theory indicates pathology, we would live in a highly pathological society. In a representative sample conducted in the Netherlands in 2009, 3% of the Dutch population believed in chemtrails.[7] This may not seem like much, but in a population of almost 17 million people, this boils down to more than 500,000 people in a small country like the Netherlands alone. These figures are hard to account for by pathology.

In fact, chemtrail conspiracy theories have been endorsed by well-known public figures who show no sign of mental illness. One believer in chemtrail conspiracy theories was the deceased musical genius Prince. He believed in a different variant of a chemtrail conspiracy theory, namely the idea that these chemicals are sprayed specifically over Black neighborhoods to harm African-American citizens and cause them to aggress against one another. In an interview with Tavis Smiley in 2009, Prince explained how as a kid growing up in a Black community he frequently saw these condensation trails in the sky and then failed to understand why people around him suddenly became aggressive. Later on, he started seeing a causal connection (patterns) between the airplane trails and the aggression that emerged. Eventually, Prince sang about chemtrails in his song "Dreamer":

> Praying that the police sirens pass you by at night?
> While the helicopter circles and the theory's getting deep
> Think they're spraying chemicals over the city while we sleep?

Naturally, the unexpected death of Prince also led to numerous conspiracy theories. Many of them asserted that Prince was murdered for telling the truth about chemtrails.

If already a sizable number of people believe a relatively absurd theory like chemtrails, how common then are more mainstream conspiracy theories, such those as about the pharmaceutical industry or the 9/11 strikes? In a nationally representative sample of the US adult population, citizens were asked to indicate their agreement with the following statement: "[T]he Food and Drug Administration is deliberately preventing the public from getting natural cures for cancer and other diseases because of pressure from drug companies." This is a statement that we cannot exclude with the same level of confidence as chemtrails, but still, it does assume an exceptionally evil mindset among a large number of medical professionals (including thousands of independent scientists and medical specialists around the world who know a few things about the actual effectiveness of these natural cures and are free to speak up). How many people believed this statement? As it turned out, 37% agreed to this statement, and yet another 31% was unsure ("neither agree nor disagree"). Only 32% of the sample disagreed.[8] As to the 9/11 strikes, in 2004 a Zogby poll revealed that 49% of New York City residents believed that US government officials knew that the attacks were coming and deliberately failed to act; and in a poll in 2006 drawn from the entire US population, 36% believed that US officials either carried out the attacks or deliberately did nothing to stop them.[9]

Conspiracy theories are far too widespread to dismiss belief in them as pathological. They are a common part of people's understanding of the world, just as various other forms of belief are. Many citizens believe that it is possible to predict the future from the lines in one's hand, or that the success of a newly formed romantic relationship depends on how well the zodiac signs of the two partners match. While these new age ideas are highly implausible in light of scientific evidence as well, belief in these ideas also is not considered pathological. Normal citizens, in all branches of society, endorse a variety of implausible beliefs, which includes certain conspiracy theories. In trying to understand the psychology of conspiracy theories, a wrong point of departure therefore would be clinical psychology (i.e., the study of mental illness). Instead, the psychology of conspiracy theories is the domain of social psychology: the study of how ordinary citizens think, feel, and act in their everyday life.

2

WHEN DO PEOPLE BELIEVE CONSPIRACY THEORIES?

"How do you explain the fact that conspiracy theories are on the rise nowadays?" This is a question that I get exceptionally often – from students, from members of an audience after giving a talk, or from journalists who are writing a newspaper article on conspiracy theories. The answer often surprises people: I don't think that conspiracy theories are on the rise. Surely there is some waxing and waning of conspiracy theories throughout the decades. In that respect I am perfectly open to the possibility that in 2016 – with Donald Trump spreading conspiracy theories during the entire US election and the UK voting in favor of a "Brexit" – conspiracy theories have received more attention than in, say, 2006. But I dispute the assertion that there is a stable trend towards more conspiracy theories in the long run. On average, the current population is not more or less conspiratorial than 30, or even 100, years ago. Scientific evidence offers little support for the idea that people have become more conspiratorial over time.

In what I regard as one of the most important, and certainly one of the most labor-intensive, studies on conspiracy theories that has been conducted so far, two political scientists from the University of Miami (helped by a team of trained research assistants) analyzed published letters that US citizens had sent to the *Chicago Tribune* and the *New York Times*.[1] The letters spanned a time period of 120 years, ranging from

1890 to 2010. Each year was about equally represented in the sample of letters, and the letters to be analyzed were randomly selected out of all the letters that were published during this period. Of primary interest to the researchers was the extent to which these letters contained conspiracy theories. In the end, these researchers read, and coded for conspiratorial content, a total of 104,803 published letters.

As might be expected, there is variation across the years in the extent to which the letters contain conspiratorial content; furthermore, in different time periods people wrote about different conspiracy theories. But over time, there was no trend upwards in the proportion of letters that contained conspiracy theories. In fact, there were two time periods that seemed to stand out in frequency of conspiratorial content, but both were not in the new millennium. The first time period when there was evidence for increased conspiratorial content was around the year 1900, during the peak of the Second Industrial Revolution. The second time period when there was evidence for increased conspiratorial content was in the late 1940s–early 1950s: at the start of the Cold War. These data clearly speak against assertions that conspiracy theories are on the rise.

Necessarily there are minor imperfections of this study that people could seize on to discredit its importance. For instance, one might reason that the letters that were actually published in these newspapers were selected by an editor and hence were not random. Some editors may have been more likely to publish conspiratorial letters than others. These are unavoidable limitations of a project like this. But we should also be realistic: This is an enormous number of letters, published in two different newspapers, selected by many different editors, over a range of a full 120 years. If there is any merit to the statement that conspiracy theories are on the rise in our modern age, there should be some trace of this visible in these data. For instance, if digital communication technologies make citizens more susceptible to conspiracy theories, the letters should show an increase in conspiratorial content starting somewhere in the early '90s and gradually increasing until the last year of measurement (2010). The data show none of this.

Also other data contradict the idea that people nowadays are more suspicious of power holders than they were about 30 years go. One study looked at the extent to which people trust and are satisfied with politicians in various EU countries over time using yearly data of the Eurobarometer.[2] Particularly the data on satisfaction are of interest, as they range from well before regular citizens had Internet, social media, and smartphones (1974) until a time when these technologies were a normal part of everyday life (2012) (the data on trust are less telling, as these ranged from 1997 to 2012 – although it is worth noting that also in these data no trend emerged suggesting a decline in trust over time). Although admittedly dissatisfaction with politicians is not the same as believing in a political conspiracy theory, one is highly likely to be diagnostic for the other: People are dissatisfied with politicians if they believe that these politicians are conspiring (and vice versa). Again, the results revealed fluctuation in the extent to which citizens were satisfied or dissatisfied with politicians, but there was no trend suggesting a drop in satisfaction levels as time progressed. Furthermore, throughout the years the average satisfaction level that citizens expressed about politicians was quite low. It would thus be a mistake to think that citizens nowadays are less satisfied with politicians than ever before. Back in the 1970s, citizens were also very much dissatisfied with politicians and, apparently, to about an equal extent as nowadays.

All of this may seem counterintuitive. After all, conspiracy theories are everywhere on the Internet and on Social Media, and these modern tools are primary means through which people learn about conspiracy theories or get into contact with other conspiracy theorists. Note that I am not saying that modern information technologies have no impact. But there is a difference between speed of dissemination and the proportion of citizens who believe conspiracy theories. My prediction would be that these modern communication technologies increase the speed through which people learn about conspiracy theories but do not increase the proportion of citizens who believe them. In a time when citizens did not have Internet or social media at their disposal, conspiracy theories were likely to spread through different, slower communication channels (e.g., word of mouth), but major conspiracy theories would spread nevertheless and ultimately reach most people anyway.

Certainly conspiracy theories spread fast nowadays. On 2 December 2015 the San Bernardino (California) shootings took place in the late morning. A married couple killed 14 people and injured another 22 with semi-automatic rifles. After the shooting, a manhunt ensued which lasted for about four hours, after which both perpetrators were killed. As the event unfolded it was evening in Amsterdam, where I was watching live coverage of this event on TV together with my wife. About two hours after the start of the shooting (and hence, two hours *before* the perpetrators were killed) I could not resist the temptation and Googled something like "San Bernardino conspiracy". Instantly various conspiracy theories came up suggesting that the shooting was a false-flag operation. We could read conspiracy theories about this terrorist attack while it was still unfolding! Without modern communication technology, however, these conspiracy theories may have reached us too, eventually – or alternatively, in Amsterdam we might not have heard about the San Bernardino shooting in the first place, and we would instead have focused more on local distressing events (leading to local conspiracy theories). Modern information technologies play a role in conspiracy theories, but when we seek answers to the question why people believe or disbelieve them, these technologies are only a piece in a much bigger puzzle.

Instead of seeking an explanation in "zeitgeist" or technology, a better and more comprehensive explanation for conspiracy beliefs can be found in psychology. I propose that conspiracy theories are rooted in a subjective psychological state that has been inherent to the human condition since the start of humanity: Conspiracy theories are a natural reaction to social situations that elicit feelings of fear and uncertainty. Specifically, the more strongly people experience such aversive emotions, the more likely it is that they assign blame for distressing events to different groups. As a consequence, we can expect conspiracy theories particularly in the wake of distressing societal events.

CONSPIRACY THEORIES AND SOCIETAL CRISIS SITUATIONS

People regularly are confronted with societal crisis situations – rapid changes in society that could potentially threaten their well-being, their way of life, or even their existence. Examples of such crisis situations are terrorist attacks, natural disasters, wars, revolutions, economic and financial crises, disease epidemics, and the like. Such crisis situations almost invariably lead to conspiracy theories. Two key examples of sudden, unexpected crises in modern history that inspired widespread conspiracy theories are the 9/11 terrorist strikes and the assassination of John F. Kennedy. Both were events that shocked society, that installed strong feelings of fear and uncertainty in people, and that gave people the feeling that the world would never be the same again. Many people have "flashbulb memories" about these events, as they still vividly recall what they were doing when they first heard the news. Both events also initiated conspiracy theories that are still being endorsed today by large groups of citizens and that many people by now have internalized as historical "facts".

The two spikes that emerged in conspiratorial content within the letters sent to the *New York Times* and *Chicago Tribune* can also be regarded as crisis situations that formed the basis of feelings of uncertainty and fear. The first spike with increased conspiracy beliefs was during the Second Industrial Revolution. During this time period major companies started to emerge, and power structures within society changed dramatically. It was a time of rapid technological progress, quick development of new infrastructure, and the efficient mass-production of a wide range of goods. Although life conditions improved for many citizens, regular laborers who were working in factories had reason for concern: There was a continuous threat of unemployment, as many jobs became obsolete after being replaced by machines. It is quite likely that these workers – who constituted a large portion of the population – experienced substantial uncertainty about their future, producing a range of conspiracy theories. The second spike with increased conspiracy beliefs was at the start of the Cold War. Shortly after the Second World War many citizens feared the prospect of a new major war, and the threat of communism was looming. As a consequence, many citizens were wary of the possibility that specific people, institutions, or groups were somehow connected to communism. This "McCarthyism" – named after senator Joseph McCarthy who was a significant figure in fueling fear of communism – was hence characterized by many (often unfounded) allegations of communist conspiracies within society. These communist conspiracy theories caused reputation damage, unemployment, and sometimes even imprisonment of people who were accused of communist sympathies.

But we do not need to restrict ourselves to the past century in order to find a connection between crisis situations and conspiracy theories. Also in the Middle Ages, examples abound of crisis situations that initiated widespread belief in conspiracy theories. Medical science was not as advanced as our current generation is used to, and it was common for young children to die of a range of dangerous diseases that nowadays are easily prevented with vaccines. Furthermore, there was no understanding of viruses or bacteria (or the importance of personal hygiene for that matter), and antibiotics were yet to be discovered. As a consequence, disease epidemics were frequent and would kill many people, but people were unable to fully understand how these diseases originated. People therefore often blamed these epidemics on people or groups in society, and such scapegoating regularly took the form of conspiracy theories. One common belief was that many young women were actually witches who conspired with the Devil to impose harm on the population such as epidemics or failed harvests. As a result of these beliefs – which are both superstitious and conspiratorial – many innocent women were burnt alive. Also the Jewish community was a frequent target of conspiracy theories suggesting that they had a causal role in crisis situations such as disease epidemics or setbacks during the Crusades, stimulating widespread persecution of Jews in Medieval Europe.[3]

These are just examples of a more general principle: In challenging times that elicit fear and uncertainty among large groups of people, conspiracy theories flourish. People start blaming people or groups that they felt uncomfortable about to begin with and come up with theories that explain the harm they experience through a malevolent conspiracy. As a result, conspiracy theories will increase in the population once there is widespread concern about a high-profile terrorist attack, a natural disaster, an economic or financial crisis, a war, a revolution, and so on. Events that pose no direct threat to peoples' own lives also can stimulate conspiracy theories, as long as it captures the attention of a large audience and causes feelings of distress among many citizens (e.g., the unexpected death of a celebrity).

In fact, even imaginary crisis situations can cause conspiracy beliefs. A case in point is the conspiracy theory that the 1969 moon landings were filmed in a TV studio. One might reason that these conspiracy theories were not a reaction to an "objective" crisis situation – it was a reaction to a positive event where humanity and science reached a new level of accomplishment. But someone who believes that the government continuously and willfully deceives the nation subjectively experiences the nation as being in crisis. Put differently, many people hold general conspiratorial beliefs about the government, and these beliefs are distressing in and of themselves, which causes further conspiracy theorizing. This is a general insight that I will return to in other chapters: Belief in one conspiracy theory stimulates belief in other conspiracy theories. In this case, citizens who hold conspiracy theories about the government are likely to approach any action of that government – including a monument to scientific accomplishment like the moon landings – with skepticism, and with additional conspiracy theories.

THE ROLE OF FEAR AND UNCERTAINTY

In order to understand why feelings of uncertainty and fear are associated with conspiracy theories, we need to establish how people cope with these negative emotions. The most common response to fear and uncertainty is to become vigilant: People start paying close attention to their environment, they start to ruminate, and they try to establish the causes of their negative feelings. Fear and uncertainty thus lead people to try to make sense of their physical and social environment.[4] Such increased sense making is an automatic response that in all likelihood is rooted in an instinct for self-preservation. Feelings of fear and uncertainty signal that there are imminent threats in the environment. Paying close attention to this environment therefore increases the chances of the organism to effectively cope with these threats and survive.

As part of this self-preservation instinct, evolutionary psychologists have noted that people tend to be risk-averse in the face of uncertain and possibly threatening situations.[5] Imagine seeing a long object in the grass, and it is unclear whether the object is a stick or a snake. In such cases, it is a natural response for people to be cautious and assume the object to be a snake. Mistakes do not have equal consequences in this situation: Someone who picks up the object assuming it to be a stick may die if it turns out to be a venomous snake. But for someone who assumes the object to be a snake and hence acts cautiously, it does not matter whether that judgment is correct or not. If one is mistaken and the snake is in fact a stick, one may take an unnecessary detour, but for the rest no real harm is done.

Feelings of uncertainty lead people to make sense of the situation that they find themselves in, and during this mental sense making it is natural for them to assume the worst. This also pertains to how people perceive others. One common finding in psychology is the "myth of self-interest". Just for clarification, this term does not mean that self-interest is a myth; of course people can be selfish from time to time. Instead, this term means that people *overestimate* the extent to which the behavior of *others* is driven by self-interest. People can be selfish sometimes, but they can also be genuinely altruistic and caring – but when trying to explain the behavior of others, people more often assume selfishness and less often assume truly benevolent motivations than is actually justified. (When Mark Zuckerberg decided to donate 99% of his Facebook shares to charity, I was astonished to read one blog after the other of people who believed him to do this out of self-interest.)

Interestingly, this myth of self-interest increases when people feel uncertain. In an experiment, participants were informed that a second participant would allocate valuable recourses between the two of them. To a varying extent, however, participants experienced uncertainty in the form of lacking information: They were not fully informed about how the allocator distributed the resources. Results showed that this informational uncertainty led participants to over-estimate the valuable resources that the allocators had given to them-selves and to underestimate the valuable resources that the allocators had given to the participants. People expected the allocators to be more selfish than they actually were, and this effect increased to the extent that people had less information about the distributions. As the authors conclude, when people lack information they "fill in the blanks" with assumptions of selfishness.[6]

This myth of self-interest is about how negatively people view other individuals, but through a similar process, feelings of fear and uncertainty also influence how negatively people view other groups in society. When making sense of the societal and political events that people encounter in their daily life, people have a tendency to assume the worst of groups that are powerful (and that could hence cause real harm), that they perceive as "different", and that they feel uncomfort-able with – such as governmental institutions, major companies, or distrusted minority groups. As a result, people come up with con-spiracy theories about the malpractice of these groups, which answers many unresolved questions that people have about the societal events that they try to comprehend. Feelings of uncertainty and fear put people in a suspicious, information-seeking state-of-mind, leading them to perceive malevolent conspiracies as responsible for a range of societal events.

Much psychological research has examined the relationship between fearful, uncertain feelings and people's tendency to believe conspiracy theories. One study was conducted in the last three months of 1999. During those months, many citizens around the world feared a major shutdown of computer systems due to the "millennium bug". This was a major issue at the time. The possibility of a millennium bug received continuous news coverage, and people feared major fallout of for instance power plants, banking systems, water supplies, and the like. If these fears had been justified and the millennium bug had become a reality, it would have had serious consequences for the economy, health care, and many other domains that directly influence the life and well-being of citizens: Anything that was run by computers would shut down. (In the end, the year 2000 started without unusual problems.) Against this background, over 1,200 US citizens responded to a questionnaire that not only asked how afraid they were for the millennium bug but also to what extent they believed in a range of common conspiracy theories. As it turned out, people who feared the millennium bug by the end of 1999 were also more likely to believe that President Kennedy was killed by a conspiracy; that the Air Force was hiding evidence that the US has been visited by UFOs; that the US government deliberately had put drugs in inner city communities; and that the Japanese were conspiring to destroy the US economy. Fear for the millennium bug was associated with belief in a range of conspiracy theories, including theories that are conceptually unconnected with the millennium bug.[7]

While these findings support the idea that feelings of fear are related with belief in conspiracy theories, they do not establish causality: We do not know whether fear of the millennium bug increased conspiracy beliefs or, instead, people who happened to believe these conspiracy theories were more likely to fear the millennium bug. In order to test for the causal order that fear and uncertainty lead to conspiracy theories, it is necessary to conduct a psychological experiment in which part of the research participants experience these distressing feelings and part of the research participants do not – and then examine whether belief in conspiracy theories is stronger among the distressed participants. Various studies tried to install these distressing feelings in participants by reminding them of situations in which they experienced a lack of control. Specifically, people have a need to feel that they are in control of whatever they do, ranging from simple movements to more complex actions such as driving a car. If people experience a lack of control they feel helpless and therefore start feeling uncertain. In a typical experiment, some of the research participants are asked to write down a specific incident in their lives where they had no control over the situation; other research participants are asked to write down a specific incident in their lives where they were in full control of the situation. After that, they are asked how plausible they find certain conspiracy theories.

Various researchers have conducted experiments along these lines, and these studies typically show that people believe in conspiracy theories more strongly when they feel distressed (e.g., because they were reminded of a situation where they lacked control) than when they do not feel distressed (e.g., because they were reminded of a situation where they had control).[8] Together with psychologist Michele Acker and a group of research assistants, we also conducted such an experiment in Amsterdam. The experiment took place against the background of the construction of a new and controversial metro line that would connect the northern and southern part of the city. Although such a metro line is likely to have many benefits once completed, it encountered severe objections among Amsterdam residents, as it would imply major construction works for years, right through the historical center. In fact, a majority of residents had voted against this project in a referendum, but the city council moved forward with it anyway. Furthermore, the construction itself ran into many problems, including being overbudget and behind schedule. Public hostility against this project reached its peak in 2009, when the construction caused unforeseen problems that posed direct harm to city residents: The underground construction had damaged the foundations of several old houses, which then had to be evacuated, as the houses literally were sinking into the ground.

When the "sinking houses" made continuous news headlines, our team of research assistants went to university cafeterias in

Amsterdam with short questionnaires and asked residents to participate in a short study in exchange for a candy bar. Participants were asked to describe either a situation from their lives where they lacked control or one where they had full control. A third group of participants were asked to describe a neutral situation from their lives, unrelated to feelings of fear or uncertainty. Then we asked participants about their conspiracy theories of the North-South Metro line: For instance, participants indicated whether they believed that members of the city council were bribed by the construction companies, whether they deliberately withheld information about the project from the public to avoid hampering its construction, and so on. In keeping with many other findings, results revealed that participants who felt fearful and uncertain (after describing a situation where they lacked control) believed these conspiracy theories more strongly than participants who felt confident (after describing a situation where they had control).[9]

In sum, feelings of fear and uncertainty fuel belief in conspiracy theories. Yet there are two complications to these effects that deserve to be noted. A first complication is that these aversive emotions do not lead to conspiracy theories among everyone and in every circumstance: Sometimes fear and uncertainty can actually *increase* support for authorities. So far we have discussed the conspiracy theories that emerged after 9/11, but we should also recognize the opposite: In the months directly after 9/11, George W. Bush was among the most positively endorsed presidents in history in terms of public approval ratings. Apparently, 9/11 not only elicited widespread conspiracy theories about the Bush administration; it also elicited massive support for the Bush administration. How can we reconcile this discrepancy with the present arguments?

The key here is that fear and uncertainty lead to conspiracy theories, but only if these theories involve powerful groups or institutions that people distrusted to begin with. Fear and uncertainty may actually increase support for powerful groups or institutions that people do trust. One study investigated whether or not the perception of leaders being moral or immoral influences belief in conspiracy theories. Naturally, people believe conspiracy theories more strongly about leaders that they find immoral than about leaders that they find moral. When people experience uncertainty, however, these effects of morality on belief in conspiracy theories become more impactful. Put differently, uncertainty makes people endorse conspiracy theories more strongly for leaders that they find immoral but less strongly for leaders that they find moral.[10] Fear and uncertainty hence do not lead to indiscriminate conspiracy theorizing; they lead people to place blame on authorities, institutions, or groups that they felt uncomfortable with from the start.

The second complication is that, often, also the "official" explanation of a crisis event entails a conspiracy. The official reading of the 9/11 strikes is that there was a conspiracy of 19 Al Qaeda suicide terrorists. Why did many citizens disbelieve this official reading and instead perceived a different conspiracy of a malevolent government performing a false-flag operation? Two interrelated issues may answer this question. First, as noted previously, when people experience fear and uncertainty, it is their natural response to be cautious and assume the worst possible explanation. In that sense, believing that 9/11 was a governmental conspiracy (and not an Al Qaeda conspiracy) is a risk-averse response: It is a lot more disturbing, frightening, and dangerous to assume that one's own government would be behind a major terrorist act, as compared to a known foreign terrorist group that is being closely monitored by secret service agencies. Second, and relatedly, a governmental conspiracy is a more grandiose explanation for 9/11 than an Al Qaeda terrorist cell: It would for instance mean that more people were involved, the level of deception would be bigger, and the scheme that was carried out would be more ingenious, and in general a government has more power than a terrorist cell. The 9/11 terrorist strikes constituted a major event in modern history, and a governmental conspiracy would be a major explanation for it. The tendency to believe a grandiose conspiracy theory may be influenced by a basic heuristic of the human mind called the proportionality bias: People have a tendency to assume that a big consequence must have had a big cause.

BIG CONSEQUENCES, BIG CAUSES?

A president is a human being, and is therefore fragile enough to die from accidents or sudden illnesses. It is perfectly possible for an otherwise healthy president to die from a tiny flu virus, just like everyone else. Now, imagine for a moment that this would actually happen to a sitting US president or a UK prime minister. Would many citizens believe that this event indeed was caused by a simple virus, or would they believe a conspiracy theory? Although certainly the opinions would differ among the public, and a lot would depend upon specific details of the case, in general I am quite confident that many citizens would come up with major conspiracy theories asserting that the president was murdered (or was kidnapped, or staged his/her own death). The explanation of an event as big as the death of a president through a cause as small as a flu virus is just hard to swallow for many people: It cannot possibly be this simple, there must be more to such an impactful, world-changing event than that. This is the essence of the proportionality bias: the assumption that a big consequence must have had a big cause.

Naturally, the unexpected death of a president would elicit strong feelings of fear and uncertainty among the population. But the proportionality bias is also broader than regulating these aversive feelings: It is a simple mental heuristic that can be seen across judgment domains, also in areas unrelated to conspiracy theories that do not elicit fear and uncertainty. Imagine two comparable students that both experience a computer crash right before having to hand in an important paper. For the first student, the consequences are disastrous: The professor fails the student for the class and does not grant an extension for the paper; this leads the student to not graduate in time and to therefore lose an attractive job offer. For the second student, the consequences are relatively small: The professor allows the student an extension to hand in the paper. As a result the student does graduate in time and can start with the attractive job. What may have caused the computer crash for the first and second student?

In a research study, half of the participants read a hypothetical scenario of the first student, and the other half read a scenario of the second student. They then selected what they thought was the most likely cause of the crash: a widespread computer virus (big cause) or a malfunctioning computer cooling fan (small cause). Research participants massively recognized a widespread computer virus as a bigger computer problem than a malfunctioning fan. But more importantly, when the consequences were big for the student, research participants were more likely to believe that the computer crash had a big cause – that is, a computer virus. These findings are unlikely to be explained by fear and uncertainty: After all, these were hypothetical scenarios of an unknown student. Instead, the proportionality bias was at work here: Participants assumed a big cause for a big consequence – in this case, a computer virus if the crash caused the student to fail his studies.[11]

The proportionality bias similarly has been shown to influence people's tendency to believe conspiracy theories. Imagine that a president of a small country gets assassinated. In one case, this assassination instigates an unforeseen chain of events ultimately leading to a war. In the other case, the assassination may still be tragic, but does not lead to a war. Put differently, the assassination has a big consequence (a war) or not. Who assassinated the president – was it a lone gunman, or was it a governmental conspiracy? A study revealed that participants considered a conspiracy more likely if the assassination led to a war than if it did not lead to a war. Again, people assumed a big cause for a big consequence, which in this case fueled a conspiracy theory. Various other studies suggest a similar principle: The more impactful and harmful a societal event is (including hypothetical ones), the more likely it is that people come up with a conspiracy theory to explain it.

Besides fear and uncertainty, the proportionality bias constitutes an additional explanation for the observation that we particularly can expect conspiracy theories in the wake of impactful, harmful societal events. Note that both the emotional explanation (fear and uncertainty) as well as the cognitive explanation (the proportionality bias) are rooted in people's desire to understand and make sense of the harmful events that they perceive in society. Sense making thus is essential in the psychology of conspiracy theories. In the following chapter, I will more precisely uncover the mental processes that are at work when people make sense of societal events – and how these may lead to conspiracy theories.

3

THE ARCHITECTURE OF BELIEF

Please get in front of your computer and Google the term "hollow Earth theory". You will find a large number of pseudo-scientific websites that make remarkable claims about the physical characteristics of our own planet Earth. As the name suggests, these theories assert that the Earth is in fact hollow. The inside of the Earth can be accessed through an entrance located at the North Pole, and all sorts of creatures live near the Earth's core – giants, an advanced race of humans, but also families of Nazis who escaped Germany after WWII. There are even more bizarre variants of the theory, claiming that we all live inside the Earth and that what seems to be the sky actually is the Earth's core. In past centuries, believing in a hollow Earth was not uncommon even among scientists, and of course, these theories were a source of inspiration for Jules Verne to write his famous novel *Journey to the Center of the Earth*. But by now, we really should know better. We have more than enough scientific evidence to be confident that the Earth is not hollow and that there are no unknown societies to be found inside our planet. Still, many people believe in a hollow Earth theory.

More generally, people believe the strangest of things despite a complete lack of evidence. Any visit to a paranormal fair will reveal groups of regular citizens – sometimes in large numbers – who firmly believe that it is possible to predict the future by reading the lines of a person's palm or by randomly drawing from a set of tarot cards. Telepathy is also accepted as possible at these fairs, assuming that one person can read the mind of a different person no matter the physical distance between them. Mediums who claim to be able to get into contact with the souls of deceased relatives (and are able to put on a persuasive performance) can earn a fortune. Also when it comes to healing illnesses, people have the – often dangerous – tendency to dismiss regular medical approaches that are based on research and evidence and instead turn to alternative approaches such as homeopathy, reiki, or spiritual healing. (This book is not the place to extensively discuss the fact that research finds no support for any of these paranormal phenomena. For readers interested in this I refer to the 2015 book by Richard Wiseman, *Paranormality: The Science of the Supernatural*).[1]

What is a belief? According to Dictionary.com, a belief is "confidence in the truth or existence of something not immediately susceptible to rigorous proof". Thus, by definition, a belief is an unproven conviction about the state of reality. Beliefs should therefore not be confused with facts. Stating that the Earth orbits the Sun is not a belief but a fact (we can measure and observe this); stating that God has a causal role in the Earth orbiting the Sun is a belief (we cannot measure or observe God). There are many qualitatively different sorts of belief pertaining to the laws of physics, religion, political ideologies, conspiracies, interpersonal relationships, and so on. Belief in a hollow Earth theory can be, and often is, a conspiracy belief (after all, a conspiracy of scientists knows that the Earth is hollow and deliberately hides the truth from the public), but it is also a pseudo-scientific belief about the physical properties of planet Earth. Belief in telepathy or hand reading are supernatural beliefs, as they suggest unknown forces of nature, but they are not conspiracy theories, as they usually do not involve a conspiracy. But people can also simply suspect that their spouse is cheating on them, which is a belief as long as they have no solid evidence to prove their suspicion.

Despite these qualitative differences, here I argue that all beliefs serve a similar function, which is to help people make sense of an uncertain situation. After all, beliefs by definition make assertions about unproven issues, that is, uncertainties. Conspiracy beliefs help people to make sense of distressing events by providing an explanation in the form of a hostile group of people pulling the strings. Belief in astrology helps people make sense of an uncertain future by making the unpredictable more predictable. Belief in the capacity of mediums to get into contact with deceased relatives helps people to make sense of what their late Uncle John has been doing recently and whether he forgives them for all the bad things they ever did to him (if we are to believe mediums, Uncle John usually does). More mundane beliefs are also about making sense of an uncertain situation, even when they are not irrational (e.g., suspecting a cheating spouse can be completely justified, but still it is a way of making sense of the behavior of the spouse – such as unusual withdrawal behavior and frequent late shifts at work). For the present purposes I will limit the discussion to beliefs that are unlikely to be true and focus specifically on a range of conspiracy theories and supernatural beliefs.

If the underlying sense-making function of conspiracy and supernatural beliefs is similar, it follows that endorsing one of these beliefs should be diagnostic for the likelihood of endorsing another of these beliefs. This certainly is the case for conspiracy theories. The best single predictor of belief in one conspiracy theory is belief in a different, unrelated conspiracy theory. The more strongly people believe that 9/11 was an inside job, the more likely they are to also believe that the pharmaceutical industry conducts illegal medical experiments in third-world countries, that CEOs of oil companies bribe politicians to start wars in the Middle East, or that scientists fabricate research data to exaggerate the perils of climate change. In fact, even beliefs in mutually exclusive conspiracy theories are positively correlated. One study has found that people who believe that Princess Diana staged her own death are also more likely to believe that Princess Diana was murdered.[2] Apparently, people who are suspicious of the death of Princess Diana are not entirely sure what happened exactly, but by seriously considering the possibility that she did not die in an accident, the door opens to a range of conspiracy theories – even the mutually exclusive ones ("I am not sure if she staged her own death or was murdered, but I do know that this was not an accident").

A common explanation for the observation that some people generally are more prone to perceive conspiracies than others is that conspiracy beliefs form a "monological belief system", or that people differ in the extent to which they have a "conspiratorial mindset". These explanations mean that believing one conspiracy theory reinforces a more general view of the world that involves the existence of malevolent conspiracies pulling the strings.[3] Put differently, if one conspiracy theory is considered true, it lowers the threshold to assume other conspiracy theories to be true as well because, apparently, conspiracies sometimes cause impactful events in the world. While compelling up to a certain extent, there is one problem that I have with this line of reasoning: Belief in conspiracy theories is also quite strongly correlated with supernatural beliefs, including the nonconspiratorial ones. Put differently, people who endorse supernatural beliefs – such as belief in telepathy, spiritual healing, astrology, and the like – are also much more likely than skeptics to believe conspiracy theories.[4] Instead of a conspiratorial mind-set, people seem to differ in the extent to which they have a "belief mind-set" that predisposes them to accept ideas for which there is little or no evidence.

The insight that conspiracy and supernatural beliefs predict one another suggests a common mental architecture. To be more precise, people can differ enormously in what they do or do not believe, but the underlying cognitive processes that lead to all of these different conspiracy and supernatural beliefs are similar. These processes are largely automatic and enable people to make sense of their environment. As a first observation, both conspiracy and supernatural beliefs are rooted in an intuitive instead of an analytic thinking style. Intuitive thinking means that people rely on their gut feelings and make judgments based on reflexive thinking and heuristics. Analytic thinking means that people carefully consider and reflect on the information that they get through complex computations. Intuitive thinking is automatic and relatively effortless; analytic thinking requires effort and concentration.

The intuitive instead of analytic basis of conspiracy theories may seem counterintuitive, given how articulate and carefully crafted some conspiracy theories are. Many 9/11 conspiracy theories are based on a seemingly elaborate analysis of how buildings are constructed, at what temperatures steel melts, and what energy is released by the impact of a passenger plane at a certain speed. I suspect that even these rather articulate theories start with the intuitive, gut-level sense that "something must be wrong" and that people subsequently search for evidence to support that sentiment. Both supernatural and conspiracy beliefs start with intuition – a fast snap judgment that a situation cannot be understood without hidden and mysterious forces. Research indicates that a tendency towards analytic thinking – and relatedly, high education levels – make people *less* likely to believe conspiracy theories and *less* likely to endorse supernatural beliefs.[5]

Belief is grounded in sense making, and this sense making takes place through automatic, intuitive mental processes. In the following, I will elaborate on the two key components of such automatic sense-making. In his 2011 book *The Believing Brain*, the well-known skeptic Michael Shermer investigates how beliefs are formed and finds evidence for two processes, which he terms "patternicity" and "agenticity".[6] These two processes mirror the first two ingredients of conspiracy theories described in Chapter 1: Pattern perception and agency detection. Both of these cognitive processes are an essential part of how the mind works and are indispensable for human beings to function normally. Specifically, sense making is all about seeing patterns and detecting agency, which human beings do continuously and automatically as they go about their everyday life. In the following, I will illuminate these two key building blocks in the architecture of belief.

PATTERN PERCEPTION

Pattern perception is the tendency of the human mind to "connect dots" and perceive meaningful and causal relationships between people, objects, animals, and events. Perceiving patterns is the opposite of perceiving randomness. Events that are random are chaotic and unpredictable; events that contain patterns, and hence are nonrandom, are understandable and predictable. The capacity of the human mind to automatically look for and find patterns is highly functional, as it enables them – among other things – to predict the consequences of their actions. In fact, I would argue that most people would not survive any single day without their ability to perceive patterns. I love jogging, and always make a conscious decision to do this in a park. Why do I never opt for a change of scenery and decide to go jogging on a busy freeway? Because I see patterns. I understand that there is a causal and meaningful relationship between cars that drive at a high speed and the likelihood of dying if one tries to jog in their way. Jogging in the park versus on the freeway differs in a nonrandom fashion in terms of expected health consequences, and the fact that people are able to appreciate that makes them better equipped to effectively navigate the world. Without being able to perceive patterns, people would be loose cannons.

Functional as it may be in most circumstances, there is one drawback to the mind's automatic tendency to look for patterns: Sometimes events truly are random, but most people perceive patterns anyway. This is referred to as *illusory pattern perception*: People sometimes see meaningful relationships that just do not exist. In fact, people are decidedly bad at perceiving randomness. Imagine being asked to produce a random outcome of a coin flip sequence (say, 100 throws; heads or tails) without being able to actually throw a coin. People fail miserably at this task, as the sequence produced by a human being trying to be random differs substantially from a truly random sequence.[7] What typically happens is that people alternate too much: After three "heads" outcomes, a human being may feel compelled to make the fourth outcome "tails" for the sequence to "appear random". But true randomness does not care about appearing random. In a random sequence, after three times of "heads" there is just another 50% chance of heads on the next throw. People therefore structurally underestimate the frequency of clusters of the same outcome appearing through a random process (say, six times with 'heads' in a row). Ironically, such clusters look like patterns to the human mind. But the truth is that this is what real randomness often looks like.

People perceive illusory patterns whenever dealing with chance or uncertain outcomes. An example of a setting where people continuously have to anticipate outcomes that depend entirely on chance is casinos. People often try and detect patterns in games such as blackjack or roulette and start betting larger sums of money if they are on a "lucky streak", switch tables if the bank has been doing well, or put their money on an uneven number if there has been an even number outcome many times in a row. In fact, research indicates that the tendency to perceive patterns in random stimuli is a good predictor of habitual gambling.[8]

Interestingly, illusory pattern perception does not appear to be exclusive to humans: Traces of illusory pattern perception has been found among pigeons. The psychologist Skinner, well known for his work on operant conditioning, provided hungry pigeons with food at regular time intervals.[9] What he found was quite remarkable: The pigeons started doing whatever they were doing shortly before they received food in the previous trial. Apparently the birds saw a pattern that was illusory, by connecting their behavior with the food that they received: "The last time I shook my head like this I received a nice treat, so let's try again." In fact, they would receive food at a fixed time, regardless of what they did. In the words of Skinner:

> The experiment might be said to demonstrate a sort of superstition. The bird behaves as if there were a causal relation between its behavior and the presentation of food, although such a relation is lacking.[10]

People have a tendency to perceive patterns in randomness, and such illusory pattern perception is part of the psychology of belief. Many events in the world co-occur through coincidence, and people tend to ascribe these coincidences to mysterious forces. If a person's house burns down after being struck by lightning, that person might for instance feel punished for having lied to his or her colleagues last week – and forgets about all the lies they told without being struck by lightning. A classic example is how one thinks of an old friend, after which an hour later that friend suddenly calls. "This can't possibly be a coincidence," so people think. But people have many old friends and therefore think about "an old friend" quite frequently. We forget about all the times when we were thinking of an old friend who did not call. Coincidences like this are bound to happen occasionally, but when they do, people fail to recognize them for what they are: illusory patterns.

Spiritual healers often use this principle to persuade the public of the effectiveness of their cures. Imagine a spiritual healer treating many cancer patients, and then one day, one of these patients gratefully contacts the healer stating that she is cured. The healer is likely to see this as evidence for the effectiveness of the cure, and therefore presents this case to the public and to medical specialists, trying to gain legitimacy for his or her approach. What the healer fails to account for is that, although rare, spontaneous remission does occur for tumors, and if the healer treats enough patients, it is actually quite likely that there will be a few of these cases among them. Even if a patient really is cured, there is no proof that spiritual healing had anything to do with it. Perhaps more importantly, the healer also fails to discount for the many patients that do not call with a thank you message, as for them the treatment did nothing to stop this terrible disease – and sometimes even prevented these patients from seeking regular medical approaches that could have saved their lives.

Also conspiracy theories are about connecting dots between events that may be entirely coincidental. Some 9/11 conspiracy theories make a big deal out of the fact that the then-Secretary of Defense Donald Rumsfeld was at the safe side of the Pentagon when the plane hit the building. "This cannot be a coincidence – he must have known that the plane was coming!" Never mind the fact that he was simply in his office when it happened, right where he would be at any regular working day. One might just as well see his presence in the Pentagon as evidence that he did not have a clue of what was about to happen: Anyone who is not suicidal and knows that a plane is about to hit a building is likely to stay far away from it. Relatedly, some conspiracy theories see a meaningful relationship between Building 7 collapsing on 9/11 and secret documents about illegal financial transactions that supposedly were stored in that building. If there really were incriminating documents in Building 7 that authorities wanted to get rid of, I can't help but wonder whether a shredder might have been a more efficient solution than hijacking four passenger planes.

An interesting research question that follows from the role of pattern perception in belief is this: Are people who are susceptible to supernatural or conspiracy beliefs generally more likely to perceive patterns in randomness? For supernatural beliefs, this question was first tested in 1985, where two researchers presented research participants with a range of probability tasks – that is, tasks in which participants had to estimate whether certain outcomes occurred by chance or through a nonrandom process (e.g., coin tosses). Disbelievers in paranormal phenomena performed better at these tasks – and hence, were better at recognizing randomness – than believers were.[11] Since then, this idea has been tested frequently, and most studies suggest that one difference between believers versus disbelievers in the paranormal is their ability to recognize coincidences.

Nevertheless, the relationship between belief and the ability to detect randomness does not emerge under all circumstances. Some studies do not find a relationship between paranormal belief and illusory pattern perception. Furthermore, researchers in France did not find a relationship between conspiracy beliefs and pattern perception.[12] This suggests that the relationship between belief and pattern perception does not emerge for all people or under all circumstances. What determines whether belief is related to a general tendency to perceive patterns in randomness? Although speculative at this point, two studies provide an interesting suggestion by finding a relationship between belief and pattern perception in regular population samples but not in highly educated samples of university students.[13] Many social scientists conduct research among university students, usually out of convenience. This does not have to be problematic in all cases, but when studying beliefs these university samples have a drawback, given that highly educated people are less likely to hold supernatural or conspiracy beliefs than less educated people. It is possible that only people who hold such beliefs above a certain threshold show a deteriorated capacity to recognize randomness.

To establish whether or not conspiracy beliefs are grounded in illusory pattern perception, I carried out a series of studies together with Karen Douglas and a student, Clara De Inocencio, on regular population samples. We found that people who saw patterns in random coin toss outcomes were also more likely to believe conspiracy theories, as well as supernatural phenomena.[14] Furthermore, we looked at the extent to which participants saw patterns in rather abstract and chaotic paintings by the American artist Jackson Pollock. These are paintings that elicit quite different reactions among modern art lovers: Some people see interesting figures or scenes in them, but others merely see paint randomly splashed on canvas. We found that the more clearly participants saw patterns in these abstract paintings, the more likely they were to believe conspiracy theories as well as supernatural phenomena. Although more research is necessary in this area, it appears that one core feature of belief is illusory pattern perception: people's automatic tendency to detect patterns in randomness.

AGENCY DETECTION

Agency detection refers to people's tendency to recognize intentionality in the actions of others. Detecting agency thus means establishing that a willful agent committed an act on purpose. As with pattern perception, people's ability to detect agency is highly functional, and in many cases lifesaving. Imagine taking a hike through a national park in Canada, and after a few hours of enjoying all the beautiful scenery you suddenly stand face-to-face with a grizzly bear. In such cases, the ability to detect agency may well save your life. Recognizing that the bear might have certain intentions (i.e., to kill you) may lead you to take appropriate action (apparently, do NOT take a run, as the bear is faster; instead, climbing a tree or staying as calm as possible, is better). Also, in many other situations it is functional to detect agency. Think of a situation where a pedestrian is killed after a collision with a car. Did the driver do this on purpose, or was it a tragic accident? People find the answer to this question crucial to establish whether or not the driver should be punished.

Agency detection is part of a broader mental capacity called "theory of mind": People are able to imagine what other people are thinking and feeling and therefore understand why others behave in a certain way. Theory of mind is indispensable to have a successful social life, because it enables people to predict the social consequences of their actions. Why do people usually not laugh out loud at a funeral? Because they have a theory of mind. People understand that unstoppable laughter upon seeing the remains of the deceased person would be extremely hurtful for all the people who are mourning. Moreover, people understand that there may be long-term consequences of such laughter. It will compromise their friendships, it will ruin their reputation, and it will decrease the likelihood that others will help them in the future. Thanks to their theory of mind, people develop a good sense of when to speak up, when to shut their mouth, when to apologize, when to turn the volume of their music a bit lower, and so on. It also enables people to understand whether an act was committed on purpose or accidentally.

But just like people make mistakes in pattern perception, they also make mistakes in agency detection: People often perceive agency where none exists. In a classic study conducted in 1944 by Fritz Heider and Marianne Simmel, participants saw two-dimensional footage of two triangles and a circle moving around on a screen and were then asked to describe what they saw. There were no computers or highly realistic animations at the time, and this footage was as basic as it gets. But that is exactly the point: Despite the fact that these utterly simplistic geometric figures clearly are not alive and have no real emotions or intentions, all participants came up with stories that ascribed agency to these figures. For instance, participants would describe how the big triangle was angry at the small triangle and became aggressive, or how the circle was curious and started nosing around the big triangle's house (which was a nonmoving rectangle on the screen). Please, try it for yourself; the footage can be found on many Internet sites, such as http://trbq.org/play/.

Have you ever been angry at the weather for giving you rain during your holiday? It takes little science education to know that the weather has no purpose and is thus not an intentional agent that one can realistically blame for anything. Rain on your holiday is just bad luck, or sometimes poor planning. Still, many people recognize the feeling of being angry at the weather, and I have experienced it as well. While some people easily recognize that ascribing agency to the weather is an illusion, many other people do ascribe the weather to purposeful agents – and for instance believe that there is a reason why they get bad weather during their holiday ("Maybe we are supposed to stay indoors and talk – we have not really talked for a while"). Detecting agency in the weather is found in all eras: Ancient societies had intentional Gods to explain the weather, such as Zeus (the Greeks) and Jupiter (the Romans) who controlled the sky, or Thor (the Vikings) who specifically determined thunder.

Many supernatural beliefs assume some sort of agency. A common assumption of many of the world's religions is the existence of one or more god(s) with motivations to punish or reward people for their actions. Belief in ghosts or in an afterlife assumes that people who have died still have agency and still are around somewhere with emotions, wishes, and desires. Fortune telling assumes that certain events are meant to happen; put differently, there is purpose in the form of a predetermined future. Finally, people often make sense of all their good and bad experiences in life – meeting a new lover, getting a new job offer, but also contracting a dangerous disease or having to suffer the death of a loved one – by asserting that "things happen for a reason"; in other words, someone or something intentionally planned all of this to happen and has reasons that we yet fail to comprehend. These are all examples of agency detection: an assumption of purpose or intention.

Agency detection is also a core feature of conspiracy theories by assuming that an act was carried out on purpose. If a plane crashes due to technical failure or human error, conspiracy theories may assert that a secret organization willfully brought it down. Or, the conspiracy theory may assume it actually was an accident, but then a secret organization still purposefully tries to cover up sensitive details such as a mysterious cargo that was on board. Conspiracy theories also rarely assume incompetence among the alleged culprits in a crisis situation. One could say that the 2008 financial crisis was at least partly due to a bad system that failed to sufficiently protect banks from human imperfections such as short-term thinking and greed. But instead, various conspiracy theories about the financial crisis assume a conspiracy of bankers who were not thinking in the short term at all but had a long-term plan to deliberately make the financial crisis happen (one example being the conspiracy theory that Democratic bankers were so impressed by Barack Obama at the Democratic convention in Denver 2004 that they deliberately caused the crisis to help him get elected in 2008). Conspiracy theories assume a sophisticated, detailed, and intelligent plan among the conspirators.

Research suggests that seeing agency where none exists is a good predictor for both supernatural and conspiracy beliefs. One study recruited university students and visitors of a paranormal fair as participants. These participants watched many short movies consisting of light points that in some cases would, and in other cases would not, jointly form a human walking figure. Participants could thus perceive or misperceive an intentional agent in these light points. Results revealed that as compared to university students, visitors of the paranormal fair reported more "false alarms" – that is, perceiving an intentional agent when in fact there was none.[15] Moreover, such illusory agency detection was a strong predictor of paranormal belief. As to conspiracy theories, one study included two measures of hyperactive agency detection. One was anthropomorphism, which refers to the tendency to ascribe human intentions and emotions to animals, objects, or situations. For instance, if one believes that the wind has emotions, one is anthropomorphizing the wind. As a second measure, research participants saw the famous Heider and Simmel footage and were asked how purposeful the shapes were. Participants who perceived more agency on both of these measures were also more likely to believe conspiracy theories.[16] Taken together, the evidence suggests that the mind's basic capacity for agency detection is part of the underlying psychology of human beliefs.

TO CONCLUDE

By describing the automatic cognitive processes of pattern perception and agency detection, this chapter was designed to illuminate what conspiracy beliefs have in common with other forms of belief. For this purpose I specifically drew a comparison with supernatural beliefs, given that like the majority of conspiracy theories, most supernatural beliefs are unlikely to be true. It should be recognized, however, that in various ways conspiracy beliefs also differ from supernatural beliefs. While many supernatural beliefs are impossible, given the laws of physics, many conspiracy theories are at least theoretically possible; and as we have seen in Chapter 1, conspiracies do occur sometimes (e.g., the Wannsee conference; Watergate). Furthermore, the five ingredients of conspiracy theories mentioned in Chapter 1 do not all apply to other forms of belief. In the next chapter, I will therefore focus on qualities that distinguish belief in conspiracy theories from other beliefs. I will specifically highlight the most central feature of any conspiracy theory: the involvement of a conspiracy, that is, a hostile, powerful, and possibly dangerous social group.

4

THE SOCIAL ROOTS OF CONSPIRACY THEORIES

On 13 November 2015, the world was shocked by the terrorist attacks in Paris. The attacks took place at multiple locations, but the largest number of casualties fell in the Bataclan theater, where a crowd of people gathered to see a concert by the band Eagles of Death Metal. Three terrorists entered the theater with AKM assault rifles and opened fire. A total of 89 people died in the Bataclan that night. The band members themselves survived the attack, although one of their employees who sold merchandise was killed. In subsequent interviews, the band members understandably were in shock about what happened. None of it was the band's fault, of course, and many people from over the world expressed sympathy for them. But that sympathy dissipated a few months later. The lead singer of the band – Jesse Hughes – proclaimed in various interviews the conspiracy theory that security staff of the Bataclan were involved in the attacks. According to Hughes, the attacks were an inside job of the Bataclan, and security staff members deliberately helped the terrorists enter the building. As a result of the allegations, various performances of the band at French festivals in 2016 were canceled, and Hughes is now no longer welcome in the Bataclan.

From a distance it is easy to judge Hughes, and his allegations indeed are ridiculous. But at least his conspiracy theories originated from real trauma. On that fateful night he had witnessed how loyal fans were shot dead from one moment to the next. He also had to run for his own life and had to mourn an employee of his band afterwards. We have seen in previous chapters that aversive emotions such as fear and uncertainty can stimulate conspiracy theories, and Hughes had every reason to experience these emotions. What is perhaps more interesting is how many people who did *not* have to run for their lives that night formed conspiracy theories about this event. The morning after the Paris attacks I checked out what had been posted at various Dutch conspiracy theorist websites. As might be expected, the web was already full of conspiracy theories, for instance accusing the French government of a "false-flag" operation. Most of these conspiracy theories were posted by people who were safely in the Netherlands, and it is a reasonable assumption that the majority of them did not know any of the victims personally.

This feature is common in many conspiracy theories: We do not have to be harmed ourselves in a particular event to believe that a secret conspiracy is responsible for it. When the Malaysia airlines Flight 370 disappeared, a host of conspiracy theories emerged throughout the world, some of them quite bizarre (in a conversation with a journalist at the time, I actually had to respond to a question about what I thought of the theory that Hollywood was behind the disappearance in order to film a real-life season of *Lost*). It is a safe bet that the vast majority of people who believe in conspiracy theories about the Malaysian airlines disappearance did not know any of the passengers on board personally. Likewise, although many people died during the 9/11 terrorist attacks, it is not a requirement to have lost a relative or close friend that day to believe 9/11 conspiracy theories. Still, not all events in the world that cause lethal casualties elicit conspiracy theories among people elsewhere in the world. On the one hand, we do not have to be harmed ourselves, or know any of the victims personally, to believe conspiracy theories; but on the other hand, not every distressing event in the world unequivocally leads to conspiracy theories.

In 1994 the Rwandan genocide took place. Within just a few weeks, militant Hutus slaughtered an estimated 900,000 Tutsis and moderate Hutus with machetes (this boiled down to about 20% of the total Rwandan population at the time). Please, take a moment to realize the meaning of this figure – almost a million innocent men, women, and children were butchered like animals within the scope of just a few weeks. One cannot compare the grief and suffering among different tragedies, but at least in terms of statistical body count, the Rwandan genocide was of an exceptional magnitude (for the sake of the argument we restrict ourselves to the killings and do not include the mass-scale raping that occurred, or the HIV epidemic that resulted from that). It is about 300 times the number of lethal casualties in the 9/11 terrorist strikes. It is 3,765 times the number of casualties in the Malaysian airlines Flight 370 disappearance (which had 227 passengers and 12 crew members on board; I assume here that they are dead, and not filming a new season of Lost on an island). It is over 6,900 times the number of casualties that fell in Paris (130 people in total). The body count of the Rwandan genocide was simply off the scale. Surely such a horrific incident must have led to major conspiracy theorizing all over the world. Right?

But when looking at European conspiracy theorist websites, it is striking how few conspiracy theories are to be found about the Rwandan genocide. To be sure, I have never been in Rwanda and can only imagine that conspiracy theories about this event are likely to be prevalent among the Rwandan population. Indeed, denial of the genocide is considered a crime in Rwanda, suggesting that there are enough disturbing conspiracy theories about this event among citizens for the Rwandan authorities to take action (likewise, denial of the Holocaust is illegal in Germany). But why do we not see website after website filled with major conspiracy theorizing about the Rwandan genocide among Europeans? One might say that the genocide took place elsewhere in the world, but this explanation is not fully satisfactory. The 9/11 terrorist strikes also did not take place in Europe, but up to this day many Europeans believe in 9/11 conspiracy theories, and they will continue to do so in the next few decades. To Europeans, both the Rwandan genocide and the 9/11 terrorist strikes were tragic events that took place elsewhere in the world. What determines how upset people are about a crisis situation, as well as the extent to which people explain the situation with conspiracy theories?

The explanation for this discrepancy can be found in a simple yet unfortunate truth about human nature: People have a tendency to categorize the social world into "we" versus "they" – and people are concerned mostly when "we" are victimized. Although Americans and Europeans love to stress how they differ, in fact their cultures are quite similar on many dimensions, and citizens regularly travel to each other's continent. When a terrorist attack occurs in the US, EU citizens experience this as if "we" are under attack (and vice versa), also knowing that next time an EU member state could be the target. Similarly, EU citizens frequently fly in airplanes and travel regularly to Australia or parts of Asia. When a flight of a modern company like Malaysian Airlines – which operates from most EU international airports – disappears under mysterious circumstances, it also feels like a highly self-relevant event for Europeans: "That could have been me, my family, or my friends on board!" Again, we can relate with the fate of the victims, even when we rationally know that the chance of being victim of a plane crash is much smaller than most other risks that we run in our everyday life. But although most Europeans are horrified by news of Hutus slaughtering Tutsis, they also perceive such an event as taking place in different world. EU citizens find it hard to imagine that such an event would happen in their own country and perceive themselves as largely dissimilar from both the victims and the perpetrators. "What happened to them is terrible – so glad that we live here."

The basic idea, thus, is that although people do not need to be victimized themselves in an event to seek conspiratorial explanations, they do need to experience an event somehow as self-relevant. Such self-relevance can be established through a sense of similarity or identification with the victims. People can also connect their identity to the victims by imagining that they themselves realistically could have been in a distressing event such as a terrorist strike – this makes the event more scary and increases people's tendency to take the victims' perspective and imagine how it must have been like for them. These perceived social connections with the victims install a desire among perceivers to make sense of the event – they get worried, ruminate, and want to find out what happened. As described in Chapter 2, these sense-making motivations lay the foundations for conspiracy theories. But when people do not connect their identity to the victims, they are less likely to experience these sense-making desires. They might be terrified by what they see – it's not that EU citizens are indifferent about genocide among Tutsis – but instead of getting worried or experiencing a desire to find out what happened, they mostly experience a desire to not have to see it. People shut down the TV or put on some cartoons and focus their attention on something else. As a result, conspiracy theories are less likely.

The distinction between "we" versus "they" also applies to the basic structure of a conspiracy theory. In a typical conspiracy theory, "they" are a conspiracy of people plotting to harm "us". A conspiracy is by definition a coalition or a group consisting of, for instance, politicians, political institutions, CEOs, major companies, ethnic or religious groups, and the like. Also, at least in the conspiracy theories that are the focus of this book, the conspiracies do not just plot against a perceiver personally – they plot against a wider collective of people, such as citizens, employees, patients, or the perceiver's ethnic or religious group. One common research finding is that the stronger people feel alienated from politics, the more likely they are to believe political conspiracy theories.[1] Why is this the case? Because people who feel alienated from politics perceive politicians as "them", "not-us". Conspiracy theories are all about "we" the victims and "they" the powerful and evil conspiracy.

This suggests that conspiracy theories are part of conflict with other groups: After all, such theories assume a different group is conspiring in order to harm one's own group. As a matter of fact, conspiracy theories are common in intergroup conflict. The ultimate form of intergroup conflict is war, and historians have noted that in virtually all wars that have been fought in recent history, both sides of the conflict had strong conspiracy theories about the enemy group.[2]

In order to understand the social roots of conspiracy theories, in the following I therefore discuss how two common characteristics of intergroup conflict relate to conspiracy beliefs. The first characteristic is the extent to which people connect their own identity to a group. The more strongly people identify with a particular group, the more concerned they are when members of that group are victimized and the less accepting they are of other, competing groups. As such, strongly connecting one's identity with a group – which for instance is reflected in feelings of nationalism, ingroup superiority, identification, and the like – may increase the extent to which people are suspicious of other groups, which inspires conspiracy theories. The second characteristic is feelings of outgroup threat. People are not worried over each and every other group simply for being different. In fact, sometimes different groups can be considered positive and useful, for instance as an opportunity for trade, or as a possible coalition partner. But in intergroup conflict, there is an outgroup that poses a direct threat to the well-being of one's own group – put differently, there is a hostile coalition, which is a central aspect of any conspiracy theory.

CONNECTING ONE'S OWN IDENTITY TO A GROUP

The previous discussion suggests a straightforward proposition about the social roots of conspiracy theories: The more strongly people connect their own identity with a particular group, the more likely they are to believe conspiracy theories when members of that group are victimized. In a series of experiments together with Leiden University Professor Eric van Dijk, we tested this basic idea.[3] We carried out a series of experiments among Dutch participants, and somewhat paradoxically, as a starting point we wanted a group or a country that Dutch participants would be unlikely to experience strong personal connections with. Ideally, our research required a country elsewhere in the world that is rarely (if ever) in the Dutch news, that Dutch people do not typically travel to, and for which our participants would be unlikely to know much of the actual culture or political situation. In the end, we came up with Benin: A small country in the northwest of

Africa. In our research study, participants would read a fake newspaper article about events that supposedly took place in Benin.

Why focus on a country that our research participants would be unfamiliar with? The main advantage of this approach is that we could start out with a group that participants do not connect their identity to, and then test what happens if we stimulate participants to become personally concerned about that group. The best test of our idea involves a comparison between people who do versus do not experience strong personal connections with a particular group – and generally speaking, it is much easier to make people connect their identity to a previously unfamiliar group than to make people feel indifferent about a group they otherwise experience strong connections with. Academic psychologists have various interventions in their research toolbox that can stimulate people to connect their own identity with a different group. One such intervention is perspective taking, a well-known method to create feelings of empathy and identification. Perspective taking means that one actively tries to understand a situation from someone else's perspective. Such perspective taking can, under some circumstances, improve relationships between different groups and reduce stereotyping.[4] In the context of our research, we told all participants that they would read a newspaper article about events happening in Benin, but we gave only half of the participants perspective-taking instructions. Specifically, we asked these participants to first for a minute try to take the perspective of the citizens of Benin and to imagine that they themselves were born and raised in Benin. They were asked to continue such perspective taking while reading the article. The other half of the participants constituted the control group. Instead of perspective-taking instructions, these participants were asked to read the article as objectively as possible.

The article that participants subsequently read portrayed a political opposition leader in Benin who was doing well in the polls and who was likely to win the upcoming elections. But then the opposition leader was involved in a terrible car crash. Here, we presented participants with one out of two different versions of the newspaper article, which varied how threatening this event would be to the average citizen of Benin. Inspired by the proportionality bias described in Chapter 2, we varied how consequential the car crash was. Half of the participants read that the opposition leader died in the crash and that the elections would be postponed until further notice (big consequences). The other half of the participants read that the opposition leader miraculously survived the crash and only had some bruises. In this latter version of the newspaper article the elections would proceed as planned (small consequences). Then, after reading the article, we asked participants about their conspiracy beliefs regarding this event. Was this accident actually an organized assassination attempt? Were the brakes sabotaged? Was the current government of Benin behind this incident?

It stands to reason that an event like this would be much more distressing to local citizens if the opposition leader dies in the accident than if the opposition leader survives. We therefore predicted that big consequences (the opposition leader dies) would lead to stronger conspiracy beliefs than small consequences (the opposition leader survives). Our results confirmed this, but conditionally so: Only participants who took the perspective of the citizens of Benin showed this proportionality bias and believed in conspiracy theories particularly strongly if the opposition leader died. Participants who were asked to be objective while reading the article did not believe conspiracy theories more strongly if the opposition leader died than if the opposition leader lived. Apparently, connecting one's own identity to a previously unfamiliar group increased conspiracy theories in response to information that this group was under threat.

In a subsequent study, we also tested why this effect occurs. We gave participants a slightly different fake newspaper article, this time about a political activist in Burundi who died of food poisoning. Our results revealed that taking the perspective of the citizens of Burundi stimulated a motivation to make sense of the event: Participants reported feeling more worried, ruminating more, feeling emotionally more involved, and having a stronger desire that the incident would be investigated thoroughly. Such sense-making motivation in turn predicted increased conspiracy beliefs, that is, belief in the theory that the activist was poisoned deliberately by a conspiracy. In sum, the more strongly people connect their own identity to a particular group, the more strongly they are motivated to make sense of an event in which a member of that group is victimized – which lays the foundations for conspiracy theories.

Connecting one's own identity with a group is a double-edged sword when it comes to morality. On the one hand, identifying with a group has many prosocial consequences. It stimulates people to help other group members, to make sacrifices on behalf of the group, and to behave in terms of the long-term collective interest instead of the short-term self-interest. Without identifying with social groups, people would only take care of themselves and their own kin. Also, there are "healthy" forms of identification that do not necessarily imply a negative perception of different groups. But on the other hand, strong personal connections with a group can take on rather pernicious forms, particularly when it involves the feeling that one's own group is superior to other groups. Specifically, people some-times may feel pride for their own group to such an extent that it reflects collective narcissism: an exaggerated belief in the superiority of one's own group. Nationalist movements often propagate ingroup superiority, typically claiming that their own country is "the greatest country on earth". Such collective narcissism can be harmful: When people believe their own group to be superior, it almost by definition implies a belief that other groups are inferior. These perceptions of inferiority may include the belief that other groups are *morally* inferior, up to the extent that they would be part of evil conspiracies to harm the "great" ingroup.

In a study conducted in Poland, two researchers investigated the relationship between collective narcissism (in this case, belief in the greatness of Poland) and people's perceptions of the Jewish community.[5] These researchers were particularly interested in the question how a belief in the superiority of Poland would predict anti-Semitism. Throughout history anti-Semitism has been widespread, and it is still prevalent at various places in the world. Anti-Semitism is closely related with conspiracy theories about Jewish people.

Examples of common Jewish conspiracy theories are that Jews all over the world conspire to achieve world domination, or that Jews have a habit of frequently conspiring to reach all sorts of malevolent goals – conspiratorial ideas that also were propagated by Hitler before and during WWII. The results of this study indicated that belief in the superiority of Poland strongly predicted such Jewish conspiracy theories, as well as beliefs that Poland is continuously under threat by other groups. These conspiracy theories and perceptions of threat subsequently predicted anti-Semitism.

In sum, connecting one's own identity to a group stimulates conspiracy theories when a member of that group is victimized; moreover, perceiving one's own group as superior stimulates conspiracy theories about other groups that are considered morally inferior. These insights underscore the social roots of conspiracy theories. An implication is that, paradoxically, conspiracy theories often are prosocially motivated: They emerge from a concern about the well-being of other group members or of the victims of a distant event, provided that perceivers somehow can relate to them. Conspiracy theories may therefore be the result of a social warning signal: a suspicious feeling suggesting that one's own community is being threatened or deceived by a hostile outgroup. But prosocial motivation does not always have prosocial consequences. If conspiracy theories about a different group are misguided, it can lead to blaming or even harming innocent people who were unlucky enough to be considered part of the suspected conspiracy.

OUTGROUP THREAT

A second proposition that follows from the social roots of conspiracy theories is that a sense of outgroup threat matters. This means that people do not form conspiracy beliefs indiscriminately about each and every outgroup: Only groups that are considered to be a threat to a perceiver's community are subject to conspiracy theorizing. This in all likelihood contributes to the fact that politicians are a frequent target of conspiracy theories. Not only do citizens often distrust the broad social category of politicians; politicians also are quite powerful and make decisions that influence the lives of many people. This is a recipe for experiencing outgroup threat: A different group is powerful and not to be trusted, making it a small step to assume that it could be conspiring to do some real harm. The same argument goes for the US government, a typical culprit in many conspiracy theories. If one feels a basic distrust of the US government, it is easy to also feel threatened by this institution: After all, the US government is powerful and could cause a lot of harm. Research indeed suggests that people particularly form conspiracy theories about outgroups that they believe to be powerful.[6]

A series of studies that were conducted in Indonesia nicely illustrate how the combination of connecting one's own identity with an ingroup along with a sense of out-group threat can produce conspiracy theories.[7] The background of these studies was how Indonesian citizens would perceive the problem of terrorism in their country. Indonesia has been targeted by various terrorist strikes in the past decades, well-known examples being the two "Bali bombings" that took place in 2002 and 2005. While these latter examples mostly targeted international tourists, various other terrorist attacks have focused on Indonesian citizens or on police officers. Having to suffer regular terrorist attacks is a likely source of fear and uncertainty among Indonesian citizens, and these events therefore increase the likelihood of conspiracy theories among the Indonesian population.

In their study, the researchers examined how Indonesian citizens would think about the following conspiracy theory: Did the terrorists who committed attacks in Indonesia conspire with Western people? This conspiracy theory portrays the Muslim community as the victim group (after all, they are not only victimized but also get the blame for the attacks) and the Western world as perpetrator group (they are really behind the attacks). In a first study, these authors asked their participants how much they identified with Muslims, to assess the extent to which participants connect their own identity to the victim group. They also asked participants to evaluate how threatening the Western world was to Muslims (an example item being "In the future, the Western world will have continued to threaten Islamic identities"). Finally, they asked participants what they thought of the theory that the Western world was behind the terrorist attacks. The results indicate that both components of intergroup conflict matter for conspiracy theories: Identification with Muslims predicted belief in these conspiracy theories, but only among participants who felt threatened by the West.

While these results are promising, they are also limited by the fact that they are correlational. Correlations show no causation: Perhaps believing in a Western conspiracy theory caused the feeling that the West is threatening to Muslims. One way to test for causality is through an experiment in which participants are confronted with information that portrays the West as either threatening or nonthreatening. These same authors therefore conducted such an experiment, again in an Indonesian setting.[8] Half of the participants read a newspaper article describing how the threat posed by Western countries to the Muslim world has been increasing in the past decades (high outgroup threat); the other half read a newspaper article describing how this threat has been decreasing in the past decades (low outgroup threat). Besides inducing a sense of outgroup threat, these authors also reminded half of their participants of their Muslim identity. These participants were requested to write a brief essay describing the nature and importance of their identity as a Muslim; the other half of the participants wrote a more neutral essay about their daily activities. Results indicated that participants endorsed stronger conspiracy theories about Western involvement in Indonesian terrorism in the high as opposed to low outgroup threat condition. This effect only occurred among participants who had written an essay about their Muslim identity, however. Put differently, the description of the West as threatening increased belief in conspiracy theories, but only among Indonesian citizens who were reminded of their Muslim identity. These findings further underscore the social roots of conspiracy theories: The combination of strong identification with one's own community and perceiving different groups as threatening make people susceptible to conspiracy theories.

MINORITY GROUPS

"The virus that causes AIDS was created in the lab in order to wipe out the African-American community." This is one out of many conspiracy theories that are popular among African-Americans, typically involving a plot by the White majority to harm or kill Black citizens. Another example is the conspiracy theory that the White majority strategically uses birth control to limit the Black population. Far-fetched as this theory might sound, in a study conducted among a random sample of 500 African-Americans, substantial numbers believed in variants of this conspiracy theory.[9] For instance, 37.4% of the sample agreed with the statement "Medical and public health institutions use poor and minority people as guinea pigs to try out new birth control methods". Likewise, 24.8% agreed to "Poor and minority women are sometimes forced to be sterilized by the government." Such conspiracy beliefs did not turn out to be harmless: They predicted negative attitudes towards contraceptives. Some of these birth control conspiracy beliefs – specifically conspiracy theories about the safety of contraceptive methods – even predicted decreased contraceptive use among men. These conspiracy theories hence increase the risk of unwanted pregnancies and STDs.

In light of the main proposition that conspiracy theories have social roots, societal minority groups provide for an interesting case. One common insight from psychology is that minority groups often are cohesive subgroups in society. Put differently, members tend to strongly connect their identity with their minority group: The group is an important part of how members see themselves, and members react strongly when they see how another member of the same minority group is victimized – think for instance of the large-scale protests following various tragic incidents where an unarmed Black suspect was shot dead by a White police officer upon arrest. A second insight is that minority group members often have good reason to feel threatened by the majority group. Members of minority groups such as African-Americans frequently face real problems such as unequal opportunities, prejudice, discrimination, poverty, and the like. Here we again see the combination of strong social ties with a group, in conjunction with a powerful outgroup that is considered threatening. What does this imply for the likelihood of conspiracy theories among minority group members?

One study compared Black versus White US college students' beliefs in a total of 13 conspiracy theories describing how the US government deliberately and selectively harms African-Americans.[10] Examples were the conspiracy theories that the government makes sure that drugs are available in Black neighborhoods; that the government deliberately creates high rates of homelessness among Black people; or that the government deliberately assigns the death penalty more to Black as opposed to White males. This study revealed that Black participants overwhelmingly believed all of these theories more strongly than White participants. Furthermore, belief in these conspiracy theories was to some extent due to the real problems that the African-American community faces. Specifically, the more strongly participants attributed their actual problems to prejudice and discrimination, the more likely they were to believe these conspiracy theories. Again, please note that many of these attributions may be justified: Prejudice and discrimination of minority groups is common and contributes to real problems such as unemployment, poverty, and crime. But when making sense of these negative life circumstances, realistic problems can easily inspire explanations that involve unrealistic conspiracy theories.

These findings underscore how the sometimes difficult relationships between subgroups in any given society may provide fertile ground for conspiracy theories. Racial tensions, or conflict between ethnic or religious subgroups, are likely to produce conspiracy theories through the features of intergroup conflict – particularly experiencing a strong connection of one's own identity with one group, in combination with perceiving the other group as a threat. While all of the groups that are involved in such conflict may endorse conspiracy theories about the other groups up to a certain extent, research on minority groups suggest that, in particular, groups that have a vulnerable position and suffer from genuine problems are highly likely to endorse conspiracy theories. After all, these groups have relatively more reason than others to experience a sense of outgroup threat, fueling a tendency to ascribe the actions of other groups to hostile conspiracies.

TO CONCLUDE

Conspiracy theories have a clear social dimension. A conspiracy by definition is a hostile outgroup, and most conspiracy theories specify how the suspected conspiracy harms or deceives a larger collective of people. In this chapter we have seen that two aspects of conflict between groups are good predictors of conspiracy theories. The closer people feel to the victims of a suspect or threatening event, the more likely it is that people explain this event through conspiracy theories. Furthermore, the more strongly people feel intimidated or threatened by other groups, the more likely it is that people will accuse these different groups of conspiracy formation. Conspiracy theories are the result of people's natural tendency to classify the world into "we" versus "they", and in an attempt to protect their own social groups from external threats, conspiracy theories place blame on the covert actions of dissimilar outgroups.

5

CONSPIRACY THEORIES
AND IDEOLOGY

The year 2016 was the year of populism. Heavily influenced by the right-wing populist party UKIP, the UK voted to leave the European Union (Brexit). Furthermore, the US elected Donald Trump as their 45th president. Both of these populist movements were characterized by a host of conspiracy theories. Researchers in the UK observed that particularly the "Leave" camp endorsed conspiracy theories during the campaign. In a poll conducted a few days before the UK-referendum, 64% of UKIP voters expected the referendum to be rigged; also, over a third of "Leave" voters believed that MI5, the British counterintelligence agency, conspired with the UK government to prevent a Brexit from happening.[1] Similarly, Donald Trump spread conspiracy theory after conspiracy theory during his campaign. He also proclaimed that the elections would be rigged; in fact, even after he won the Electoral College, he continued claiming that Democrats only won the popular vote through foul play. Moreover, he proposed that climate change is a "hoax perpetrated by the Chinese", maintained for years that Obama was not born in the US and hence should have never been president, seized on every opportunity to implicate Hillary Clinton as part of a conspiracy (e.g., "The Clinton foundation is the most corrupt enterprise in political history"), proposed that vaccines cause autism, and so on. Quite plausibly, these populist movements had electoral success not despite, but because of, their public endorsement of conspiracy theories.

In the wake of Brexit and Trump, I have little trouble persuading my academic colleagues that conspiracy theories are prevalent on the political right. But, in fact, conspiracy theories are prevalent at the political left too. Democrats also endorsed a number of conspiracy theories (e.g., allegations that Trump colluded with Putin and WikiLeaks to influence the elections). In studies conducted in the EU, I frequently find that the political left also is conspiratorial, although often about different topics than the political right. Examples of EU left-wing conspiracy theories pertain to wars (e.g., Iraq), major companies, the US government, and so on. Examples of EU right-wing conspiracy theories pertain to science (e.g., climate change), immigration, terrorism, and other topics that the political right typically is suspicious of. The left and right also share conspiracy theories about a range of topics, such as politicians in general and the role of the EU in local policy.

This is not to say that there are no psychological differences between people with left-wing versus right-wing political ideologies. Many political psychology studies identified a number of noteworthy psychological differences between the left and right that are now well established within the scientific community. For instance, the political right tends to be more authoritarian than the political left, which means that right-wingers have a stronger desire for order as reflected in a tendency to require rule following and an aversion towards counter-normative outsiders. The political right also scores higher on a variable called "social dominance orientation," which refers to a willingness to accept inequalities between groups.[2] But besides a distinction between left and right, another meaningful distinction within political psychology is between political extremes and moderates: In many ways the extreme left and extreme right resemble each other closely and differ from people who are politically moderate.

For instance, the political extremes – at both the left and the right – tend to be rather confident of their political beliefs, yet they also share a pessimistic outlook on an uncertain future. In one study, the political extremes reported feeling more uncertain about their economic future than moderates were and, for instance, worried that there would be little pension for them when they were old, or that in the near future the Western world would be set back to a much lower level of prosperity. Also, compared to moderates, the political extremes tend to be less tolerant of groups that they perceive as different – implying that the extreme left derogates groups such as bankers, millionaires, and soldiers, and the extreme right derogates groups such as Muslims, gay and lesbian people, and scientists. An additional study suggests that besides being less tolerant of different groups, the political extremes at both sides of the spectrum are also less tolerant of people holding different opinions than themselves and are more likely to agree with statements such as, "People who think differently than me about political issues are of lesser value than I am" or "It scares me if people think differently than I do about political issues."[3]

In modern democracies, the political extremes are typically embodied by populist movements in parliament. In that sense, I find it remarkable how even established political psychologists tend to mention the word "populism" in the same breath as "right-wing" – assuming that right-wing ideologies are a defining characteristic of populism. In fact, populism is not an ideology but a way of thinking that construes politics as a struggle between "the people" versus "the elites".[4] As such, populism can occur across the political spectrum, although it is most common at the political right *and* left extreme. Populist parties essentially presume to speak on behalf of the people. Underlying dimensions that follow from such people-centrism are anti-elitism (i.e., populist parties typically have an aversion against the political elites, and sometimes also against societal elites such as scientists, CEOs, or bankers), anti-pluralism (i.e., populist parties assume that only they represent the true voice of the people, and are therefore less accepting of dissenting opinions than moderate parties), and threatened nationalism (i.e., populist parties propagate pride in one's country, along with the notion that the country is headed into the wrong direction).

In the US, such populism arguably is more pronounced at the political right (the Tea Party; Trump), although it also exists at the political left (e.g., the "Occupy Wall-Street" movement). Populism likewise appears to be more common at the political right in Western Europe, although the EU also has a number of left-wing populist movements. Examples of EU right-wing populist parties are UKIP (UK), Front National (France), PVV (the Netherlands), and AfD (Germany). Examples of EU left-wing populist parties are Podemos (Spain), Syriza (Greece), Die Linke (Germany), and SP (The Netherlands). But in large parts of Latin America populism is more common at the political left, a prime example being Hugo Chavez – after his death followed by Nicolás Maduro – in Venezuela. Other examples of countries with strong left-wing populist movements are Ecuador, Bolivia, and Brazil.

It remains speculative why countries differ in whether extremism or populism is mainly a right-wing or a left-wing phenomenon. A plausible reason is a combination of cultural differences and social-economic circumstances that make citizens of different countries concerned about different types of threat. For instance, it has been argued that right-wing populist movements are more successful in Northern European countries because, due to their wealth, these countries are attractive to immigrants. Relatedly, left-wing populist movements have been relatively successful in Southern European countries, which might be due to the fact that these countries face more substantial economic problems and suffer more from austerity measures than other EU member states.[5]

My point in this chapter is that conspiracy theories are more likely among people who endorse extremist or populist beliefs, and such extremism can occur on both the political left and the right. The underlying psychological features of extremist beliefs provide exceptionally fertile ground for conspiracy theories. For instance, if one has an aversion against societal elites, it is a small step to assume that those elites are involved in hostile conspiracies. Moreover, extreme ideologies tend to be nationalistic, and we have seen in Chapter 4 how nationalist sentiments exacerbate conspiracy theories. Finally, extremists are more uncertain about their economic future than moderates are. It is therefore not a coincidence that extremist and populist leaders often have strong appeal to parts of the population by virtue of their clarity. Populist politicians use catchy one-liners and therefore are praised for "telling it like it is". But in fact they propose simplistic solutions for the relatively complex problems that a country faces. Endorsing populist leaders may hence originate from a desire for clarity – and such clarity is also provided by conspiracy theories. After all, conspiracy theories offer comprehensive explanations for complex events, and we have seen in previous chapters how conspiracy theories flourish in particular in uncertain situations.

In the following, we first examine how common conspiracy theories are in nondemocratic, suppressive extremist regimes, both at the extreme left (communism) and the extreme right (fascism). After that, we review studies that have investigated the link between political ideology and conspiracy theories among citizens living in modern democracies. These latter studies specifically tested whether citizens who ideologically are at the edges of the political spectrum – radical socialist party voters as the populist left and anti-immigration party voters as the populist right – are more susceptible to conspiracy theories. Finally, we will discuss conspiracy theories among members of extremist fringe groups in society – some of them violent – specifically focusing on religious-fundamentalist, political extremist, or other ideologically extreme groups.

CONSPIRACY THEORIES IN EXTREMIST REGIMES

Cuba is under strict communist rule and belongs to the most repressive regimes in the world. In 2009 I had the opportunity to travel to this country for a few weeks. Traveling to Cuba was one of the most interesting and rewarding experiences in my life, and I was struck by the beautiful sceneries on the one hand but also by the widespread poverty on the other. At first blush the population appears cheerful, with lots of singing, music and dancing; but just below the surface, one can feel the excessive control that the regime exerts on their lives. For instance, I have found Cuban citizens very reluctant to talk about the political situation in their country, reflecting an awareness of the possible consequences of voicing one's opinion about the regime. In Havana, I visited the well-known *Museo de la Revolucion*, where I saw the following statement presented as a historical fact:

> A bacteriologic aggression of the CIA introduced in our country the virus of dengue or breakbone fever. Out of 344,203 known cases, 116,115 were hospitalized; 57 adults and 101 children died.

Dengue fever is a terrible infection indeed, but it is common in countries with a tropical climate. It occurs in all other countries within the Caribbean, and also in large parts of Central and South America, Africa, India, and Southeast Asia. At present dengue fever occurs in

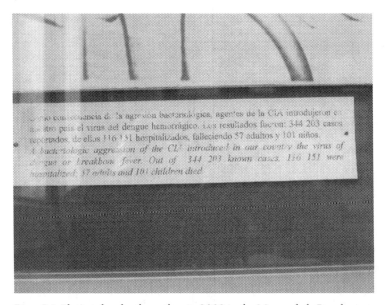

Figure 5.1 Photo taken by the author in 2009 in the Museo de la Revolucion; Havana, Cuba.

more than 110 countries worldwide. There would be no need for the CIA to introduce it in Cuba, as Cuba's climate would have attracted the mosquito that carries the virus anyway. But in 1981 Fidel Castro publicly accused the United States of introducing this disease in Cuba, and as the museum statement suggests, in 2009 the Cuban authorities still blame the occurrence of this disease in their country on a conspiracy of their arch-enemy (it is yet unclear to me why the museum labeled the supposed aggression "bacteriologic" given that dengue is, as acknowledged by the statement itself, a virus).

Is it a coincidence that such a conspiracy theory would be formally propagated within a country ruled by an extremist regime? Let me start out by saying that it is difficult to conduct social-psychological research in countries ruled by suppressive extremist regimes – even if researchers would get the opportunity to interview citizens, it is highly questionable whether those interviews would elicit reliable responses reflecting citizens' true beliefs instead of citizens' expectations of what the regime wants to hear. But we do know a lot about extremist regimes and the role of conspiracy theories in them, through historical sources. One key insight that emerges from these sources is that conspiracy theories are highly common – at least among the ruling powers – in both communist (extreme-left) and fascist (extreme-right) regimes. Typically, leaders of such regimes spread conspiracy theories about enemy groups or dissenting ideologies to gain support for their cause. Furthermore, such regimes have a fear for conspiracies, as reflected in continuous monitoring of citizens and prosecuting people for having apparent ties with countries or ideologies that are considered the enemy.[6]

Back in the 1930s and early 1940s, Adolf Hitler gave numerous speeches in which he expressed his hatred for Jewish people. Also in his book, *Mein Kampf*, he took the time to elaborately illuminate the reasons for his anti-Semitism. Why did Hitler hate Jews so much? If one looks closely at his argumentation, part of the answer seems to be that Hitler was a convinced believer in Jewish conspiracy theories. He blamed the German defeat in WWI, as well as the rapid economic decline that followed, on a Jewish conspiracy. Also, he believed that both communism *and* capitalism were the result of Jewish conspiracies for world domination. It needs little argument that Hitler's conspiracy theories had enormous and tragic consequences. His Jewish conspiracy theories gave the German population a convenient scapegoat for their problems, which facilitated Hitler's rise to power. Furthermore, the conspiracy theory connecting Jews to communism – referred to as "Judeo-Bolshevism" – was a central argument not only to initiate the Holocaust but also to invade Stalin's Soviet Union. Of course, there was no Jewish conspiracy behind communism. In fact, Joseph Stalin himself also believed Jewish conspiracy theories and held a Jewish conspiracy responsible for the rise of Nazism.

Once in power extremist regimes typically suppress dissent and prohibit a free press. One of the main reasons for such a restricted freedom of speech among citizens is a fear of conspiracies. Dissenting citizens are often regarded as undermining the state and are accused of conspiratorial activities to harm or overthrow the regime. It is well known that Joseph Stalin ordered thousands of people to be executed because of fear that they might be forming conspiracies against him and his administration. Likewise, in former East Germany the KGB spied on thousands of citizens. During these activities the KGB was particularly interested in the extent to which citizens privately held critical opinions about the regime, which was considered to be an indicator that citizens were enemies of the state who were conspiring against the regime. Moreover, the KGB paid particular attention to the possibility that citizens were colluding with the "imperialist West". Even the most remote connections with the West, or with political dissidents sympathizing with the West, could get citizens into serious trouble. The key here is a fear of conspiracies among citizens that could somehow erode the regime's power.

Conspiracy theories hence have been and still are prevalent among the repressive extremist regimes that our world has seen. Although it is difficult to establish how much regular citizens who are living in such regimes endorse conspiracy theories, the ruling extremist parties typically express strong conspiracy theories. They propagate conspiracy theories about countries, ideologies, or societal groups that they consider to be hostile. Furthermore, extremist regimes are continuously suspicious of their own citizens and easily prosecute political opponents, dissidents, or regular citizens under the accusation of state-undermining conspiratorial activities.

CONSPIRACY THEORIES AND POPULISM

While it is difficult to ask citizens of suppressive regimes to fill out questionnaires asking about their belief in conspiracy theories, in modern democracies where citizens are free to criticize whomever they like, such research is relatively easy to conduct. An interesting question, therefore, is whether in modern democracies people at the political extremes are more likely to believe conspiracy theories than political moderates. Before we start, I should note that one should be careful not to equate citizens in, for instance, the EU or the US who ideologically are at the edges of the political spectrum with the suppressive regimes discussed previously. In fact, I can get bothered by people who portray EU anti-immigration parties as "Nazis" or EU socialist parties as "communists" – such characterizations are over-simplifications that ignore important historical differences and fail to recognize the extent to which such dictatorial regimes have slid down a moral slippery slope. For instance, current anti-immigration parties typically are protectionist (i.e., they want to better protect their country's existing borders) whereas the Nazis were expansionist (i.e., they wanted to *expand* Germany's borders), rendering obvious differences in the inevitability of war. Likewise, modern EU socialist parties favor democracy and referenda, this in stark contrast with suppressive communist regimes. These differences notwithstanding, the theory laid out in this chapter of how ideology and conspiracy theories are connected should also hold for populist movements in democratic countries. In the following paragraphs we do not compare democratic systems versus nondemocratic regimes; we compare populist versus moderate voters within modern democracies, and given the characteristics of populism I propose that we should find a relative difference between populists and moderates in conspiracy theorizing.

A first test of the relationship between extreme political beliefs and conspiracy theories was conducted by the political scientist Ronald Inglehart, who analyzed data from the Eurobarometer survey of 1984, carried out in six nations (Germany, Italy, the UK, France, Belgium, and the Netherlands).[7] He specifically looked at participants' self-placement on a scale ranging from the political left (1) to the political right (10), as well as participants' responses to the question how much they distrusted their nations' courts of law. What he found was a "U"-curve: The more extremely participants scored on political self-placement (that is, towards the left or the right end of the scale), the more they distrusted their nation's court of law. People who were in the political center were least likely to distrust their nation's court of law. Inglehart also looked at the country level and found that the U-curve materialized for 5 out of 6 nations (the exception being France, where the political right was more distrustful of the courts than the political left – Inglehart explains this anomaly by the notion that radical left-wing parties were in power in France during the early 1980s, leading right-wing people to perceive the courts as ideologically biased).

Inspired by Inglehart's findings, I also conducted a series of studies on the relationship between ideology and conspiracy theories, together with political scientist André Krouwel and psychologist Thomas Pollet. One limitation of Inglehart's findings is that his study did not assess conspiracy theories directly: His dependent measure was distrust in courts of law, and people can distrust courts of law also for nonconspiratorial reasons. For instance, a person may believe the courts to be incompetent, or a person may believe that the courts of law are simply indifferent about doing justice – beliefs that lower the trust that people have in the justice system but that do not qualify as conspiracy theories, as these beliefs do not involve hostile and secret coalitions. Two of the studies that we conducted were nationally representative samples of the Dutch voting population. We asked participants' belief in a range of conspiracy theories, some of them politically neutral (e.g., beliefs about the extent to which politicians have connections with organized crime), some of them more plausibly endorsed by the political left (e.g., beliefs about the role of oil companies in waging war against Iraq) and some of them more plausibly endorsed by the political right (e.g., beliefs about how scientists deliberately exaggerate climate change). Our results revealed the same U-shape as Inglehart: Participants who placed themselves at either the extreme left or the extreme right were on average more likely to believe conspiracy theories than participants who placed themselves in the political center.[8]

We also conducted a study in the US, in which the results revealed the U-curve for conspiracy theories about the financial crisis (e.g., beliefs such as that the government profited from the crisis in ways that the public is unaware of or that the crisis was caused by a conspiracy of bankers and corrupt politicians). Furthermore, we examined theories suggesting that a conspiracy deliberately exaggerates the perils of climate change, but these conspiracy theories were endorsed mostly by the (extreme) right – which makes sense, as the left and right differ in how concerned they are about climate change. Of further interest was what happened on a measure of personal paranoia: Beliefs that others have bad intentions towards or even conspire against a perceiver personally (measured through participants' endorsement of statements such as "I sometimes feel as if I am being followed", or "Some people have tried to steal my ideas and take credit for them"). On such personal paranoia, the extremes did not differ from moderates. Apparently, people who are politically at the left or right extreme are more conspiratorial than political moderates, but only about topics that concern the collective interest such as a financial crisis, a war, or politicians in general. They are not more likely than moderates to believe that people are conspiring against them personally. The political extremes are more suspicious than moderates about societal and political events, not about the people that they encounter in their own personal lives.

A recent study in Germany also found stronger conspiracy theorizing among the populist left and right than among moderates.[9] This study looked at how party preference would predict an individual difference variable called "conspiracy mentality". Conspiracy mentality reflects a generalized tendency to perceive conspiracies in the world, assessed by asking whether participants agree with general conspiratorial statements such as, "There are secret organizations that have great influence on political decisions." This study revealed that conspiracy mentality was again highest at the political extremes: Specifically, voters of the German radical socialist party (i.e., the populist left) and voters of German anti-immigration parties (i.e., the populist right) scored highest on conspiracy mentality. Conspiracy mentality was lowest among people voting for centrist, mainstream parties.

In sum, conspiracy theories flourish particularly among people at the edges of the political spectrum in modern democracies – specifically, the populist left and the populist right. More evidence is needed from different countries, however. One might for instance speculate that conspiracy theories are relatively more pronounced at the political left in countries where the left tends to be more radical (e.g., parts of Latin America) and relatively more pronounced at the political right in countries where the right tends to be more radical (e.g., the US). Furthermore, conspiracy theories are influenced by the question of who is in power at a given point in time. Political scientists have noted that conspiracy theories about the government are less likely among people who voted for the ruling parties than among people who voted for opposition parties.[10] These complexities notwithstanding, the evidence suggests that, in democratic societies, conspiracy theories are particularly common among people with politically extreme beliefs.

EXTREMIST FRINGE GROUPS

The previously mentioned studies were conducted on samples of regular citizens and found differences in conspiracy theories between people voting for populist parties as opposed to people voting for relatively moderate parties. The populist parties that we discussed take part in the democratic process by participating in national parliaments, however, and are endorsed by a sizable portion of regular citizens. How about fringe groups that are much more extreme, often break the law, and sometimes are prone to violence? Think of underground groups of neo-Nazis or White supremacists (far right), anti-globalization extremists or communist revolutionary groups (far left), and also religious extremist groups such as Al Qaeda, Islamic State, Christian anti-abortion extremists, or cults. How prevalent are conspiracy theories among members of such extremist fringe groups in society? Also, what specific role do conspiracy theories play in such groups – specifically, do conspiracy theories inspire violence among their members?

As with suppressive extremist regimes, doing research among members of such extremist fringe groups using standardized psychological questionnaires is a difficult, if not impossible, task. First, one would need to find members of such fringe groups *and* find them willing to participate in research, which may already prove to be quite a challenge, particularly for the groups that commit crimes and are prone to violence. Second, even if one would find a few members of such groups willing to participate in research, it is questionable that one would find enough members to conduct psychological survey research, as such research is quantitative: Participants' responses to questionnaires are analyzed with statistical analyses, and in order to for these analyses to be meaningful one needs a substantial sample size (the exact required sample size depends on a number of issues such as the number of variables examined and the effect size to be expected, but as a rough indication, one would easily need 200 participants at a minimum). Thus, quantitative research methods are difficult if one aspires to study these fringe groups.

Various qualitative research methods do not require these sample sizes, however. One interesting study, conducted by Jamie Bartlett and Carl Miller, analyzed over 50 extremist fringe groups in the UK, Europe, and the US through qualitative research methods.[11] These researchers specifically looked if, and to what extent, conspiracy theories were mentioned in the official documents or recorded speeches of each group. The study included a host of religious extremist groups, including Al Qaeda, Hamas, Army of God, Lambs of Christ, Jewish extremist groups, and various cults such as "Peoples Temples"; the study also included far-right groups such as Aryan Nations, the Ku Klux Klan, the British People's Party, and various right-wing militias; at the far left the study included groups such as the Angry Brigade, the Red Army Faction, and anti-globalization extremism; and the study included a few ideologically extreme groups that could not clearly be classified on a political left-right dimension or as a fundamentalist religious group, such as anti-technology extremist groups, the "Committee for Liquidation of Computers" (a violent group that was responsible for attacks on various computer centers in the early 1980s), and revolutionary political groups that combat both communism and capitalism.

Surely such a diverse array of extremist fringe groups – some of them ideologically more bizarre than others – cannot have much in common. Or can they? At least one factor seemed to connect most of these groups, which was the observation that their formal documents and the recorded speeches by their group leaders contained conspiracy theories. To be sure, not every fringe group in this study had documentation showing clear and straightforward evidence of conspiracy theories – for instance, the researchers did not find conspiracy theories in the documents of the "Real IRA". But for the vast majority of the groups that were under investigation, these researchers observed conspiracy theories in their documentation. There were subtle differences in the conspiracy theories that the groups adhered to, with some groups believing that Jewish conspiracies control world governments (far right), others believing in a Western conspiracy to destroy Islam (e.g., Al Qaeda), and again others in a conspiracy of financiers and bankers to have excessive power over the world (far left), to name a few. But there were also many resemblances across these groups, such as a frequently recurring belief in a totalitarian world government (e.g., a "New World Order"). As concluded by the authors of this study, "It is striking that there is considerable overlap and fusion between many of these conspiracies, even across groups that exist at opposite ends of the ideological spectrum" (p. 4).

Some of the extremist fringe groups under investigation were violent, and others were not. Was there a difference between violent versus nonviolent fringe groups? These researchers found that conspiracy theories occurred among both the violent and the nonviolent groups. It would therefore be too easy to conclude that conspiracy theories necessarily lead to violence: Although conspiracy theories can sometimes inspire extremist violence such as terrorism, they do not have to. Instead, Bartlett and Miller conclude that conspiracy theories work as a "radicalizing multiplier": Conspiracy theories exacerbate the dynamics underlying extremism, thereby accelerating the process of radicalization. Furthermore, they can contribute to the process through which groups that already are ideologically extreme subsequently turn violent. Put differently, conspiracy theories make groups ideologically more extreme, and only once this extremism has reached a certain point can conspiracy theories subsequently also contribute to these groups turning violent.

Bartlett and Miller highlight three more specific processes through which conspiracy theories act as a radicalizing multiplier, and only the third and final process describes how conspiracy theories can turn an extremist group violent. The first process is that conspiracy theories demonize outsiders. Extremist fringe groups make rather sharp distinctions between "us" versus "them", and conspiracy theories enable these groups to solidify a strong identity among their members by fueling aversion against different groups. The second process is that conspiracy theories enable extremist groups to discredit criticism of the group. Dissenting voices may threaten the cohesion of extremist groups, but conspiracy theories enable these groups to portray critics as part of a hostile conspiracy. And third, conspiracy theories can give extremist fringe groups the feeling that violence is the only remaining option. More specifically, conspiracy theories can add to the sense that the group – or the cause that the group stands for – is under imminent attack by a hostile conspiracy, that there is an urgent need for an adequate response, and that a peaceful reaction is unlikely to be effective.

While these ideas are compelling, more research is needed to more clearly test the causal order that the "radicalizing multiplier" suggests. Specifically, the study's analysis implies that conspiracy theories lead to radicalization, but to have more confidence in this conclusion, we need more straightforward evidence about causality. For instance, does excessive belief in conspiracy theories predict the extent to which a person has radicalized a year later? At present we cannot conclude with certainty whether conspiracy theories cause radicalization, whether radicalization causes conspiracy theories, or whether conspiracy theories and radicalization mutually reinforce each other. What does seem clear, however, is that conspiracy theories are part of the entire process of radicalization: They play a role in the dynamics that turn people from moderate into extreme and in the dynamics that make extremist people resort to violence.

TO CONCLUDE

In the present chapter we examined the link between ideology and conspiracy theories and found that belief in conspiracy theories is prevalent particularly among people who endorse extreme ideologies. This conclusion follows from three sources of evidence. First, historical evidence suggests that conspiracy theories are a central part of suppressive, dictatorial extremist regimes. Second, research from political psychology reveals that in modern democracies, populist voters are more likely to believe conspiracy theories than people who vote for moderate, mainstream parties. And third, a qualitative analysis of extremist fringe groups suggests that, independent of ideological content, conspiracy theories are common among such groups. Conspiracy theories are intrinsically linked to a polarizing political climate, where different ideological groups portray opposing groups as enemies.

6

EXPLAINING AND REDUCING CONSPIRACY THEORIES

After an interview about conspiracy theories for the local journal of my university, the journalist asked if I would mind having my picture taken while wearing a tinfoil hat. Slightly off-guard, I agreed, and considered it a good joke at the time (although admittedly I might have reconsidered had I known that the picture would end up on the journal's front cover). But later on I thought more carefully about this request, and realized that it reflects the stereotypical image that many people have of conspiracy theorists: socially awkward individuals who have lost all touch with reality and believe rather outrageous theories such as that tinfoil hats would protect them from the radiation that the government uses to manipulate their brains. Some of the theories discussed in this book indeed are exceptionally bizarre, ranging from alien lizards to chemtrails to hollow earth theories.

But these bizarre theories notwithstanding, such "tinfoil-hat" characterizations do not do justice to the societal phenomenon of conspiracy theories, nor to the people who believe in them. While the number of citizens who believe conspiracy theories such as alien lizards or chemtrails is surprisingly high, it still is a small minority of the total population. More important is how widespread many "mainstream" conspiracy theories are, such as that the 9/11 terrorist strikes were an inside job, that climate change is a hoax, that the pharmaceutical industry spreads dangerous illnesses, and so on. One does not need to be socially awkward or out of touch with reality to believe these mainstream conspiracy theories. On the contrary, large portions of normal, law-abiding, well-functioning citizens believe these conspiracy theories. Furthermore, while conspiracy theories are slightly more common in the lower educated segment of society, they are by no means exclusive to this segment, as they also emerge among high-profile managers, actors, scientists, lawyers, and even the current US president, Trump. Conspiracy theories are a common part of public discourse, and we do not need to go online to learn about them, as we can also hear them in bars, at parties, on the streets, in public transport, at the grocery store, and so on.

Why are conspiracy theories so widespread? In this final and concluding chapter, I will first summarize the insights of the previous chapters in an effort to understand conspiracy theories as a common societal phenomenon. One of the main mistakes that one can make in explaining conspiracy beliefs is to dismiss them as pathological. Instead, my conclusion will be that conspiracy theories emerge from regular and predictable psychological responses to feelings of uncertainty and fear. After my conclusions about the psychology of conspiracy theories, I will raise a few suggestions as to what policy makers can do to reduce conspiracy theories among the population.

WHY ARE CONSPIRACY THEORIES WIDESPREAD?

Negative emotions – particularly feelings of fear and uncertainty – form a key causal factor to explain why conspiracy theories are prevalent among large segments of the population. These negative emotions explain why conspiracy theories flourish in the wake of societal crisis situations. This includes both sudden crises such as terrorist strikes, natural disasters, or the unexpected death of a public figure and ongoing crises such as climate change, epidemics, or wars. But also in the absence of an unambiguous and objectively real crisis event, negative emotions can cause conspiracy theories. Uncertainty about the future, feelings of alienation, fast-changing power structures in society, rapid technological advancement, or a deep-rooted distrust towards formal authorities can all stimulate conspiracy theories. Negative emotions elicit sense-making processes in which people assume the worst, increasing people's suspicious feelings towards powerful, dissimilar, or distrusted outgroups. These suspicious feelings can be dissected in a range of more specific psychological processes that characterize conspiracy theories and that can be summarized in terms of the following three complementary insights.

INSIGHT 1: CONSPIRACY THEORIES ARE ROOTED IN A DISTORTION OF COMMON AND FUNCTIONAL COGNITIVE PROCESSES, NOTABLY PATTERN PERCEPTION AND AGENCY DETECTION

People perceive patterns and detect agency, and these are highly functional properties of the human mind. Without our ability to perceive patterns we would be unable to distinguish the good from the bad, the healthy from the poisonous, or the safe from the dangerous. Pattern perception is all about the human capacity for associative learning: Through experience and observational learning we develop causal theories about the world that often are correct and that enable us to predict the consequences of our actions – such as that we might break our leg if we jump off a high roof or that we might regret smoking a cigarette while filling our car with gasoline. Furthermore, without the ability to detect agency, people would be socially helpless. Agency detection enables us to establish whether people performed certain acts on purpose or not, and it helps us to predict the future behavior of others by understanding their intentions. By correctly recognizing agency we can tell when others are flirtatious, aggressive, or just accidentally looking our way. Accurate agency detection also prevents us from being terrified each time we see a strange shadow and makes us able to estimate when a barking dog can be safely hugged or should be approached with caution.

Feelings of uncertainty and fear, however, cause an activation – and frequently, an overactivation – of the human tendencies to perceive patterns and detect agency. People sometimes perceive patterns in what actually are coincidences, and feelings of fear and uncertainty exacerbate such illusory pattern perception. Studies for instance show that when people lack control, they not only start seeing conspiracies, but they also start seeing patterns in other stimuli, such as images in random noise, patterns in stock market information, and superstition.[1] Likewise, people frequently detect agency where none exists, as indicated by the classic study by Heider and Simmel in which all participants ascribed agency to simple geometric figures on a screen. Feelings of fear and uncertainty stimulate the human tendency to detect agency, which may result in conspiracy theories, or in other beliefs that assume agency. For instance, under conditions of fear and uncertainty, people believe more strongly in personified, agentic gods.[2]

The cognitive processes underlying conspiracy theories hence are not pathological; they are regular processes that our minds perform continuously and that get more strongly activated as a response to uncertainty and fear. In many situations, the relationship between uncertainty and activation of these cognitive modules can be functional, too: When there truly is danger, pattern perception and agency detection help people to find out the nature of the threat and take appropriate action. One reason why conspiracy theories are widespread among regular citizens, therefore, is because they involve normal and otherwise functional cognitive processes.

INSIGHT 2: CONSPIRACY THEORIES ARE ROOTED IN PERCEIVED INTERGROUP CONFLICT

Humans are social beings. People have a natural tendency to affiliate with others and have a fundamental need to belong to social groups. The power of this "need to belong" becomes apparent particularly when people are excluded by others or by groups that they value – a romantic breakup, a rejection by people previously considered to be friends, or a denial to attend a party that everyone else is invited to. Such social exclusion ranks among the most aversive experiences in life, which undermines self-esteem and lowers the feeling that one belongs, that one is in control, and that life is meaningful. Social exclusion hurts – in fact, neurological evidence suggests that experiencing exclusion activates the same brain regions as experiencing physical pain does.[3] Why is social exclusion so painful? Because it is in our nature to desire having meaningful social relationships with other people, and social exclusion forms a threat to this desire. Instinctively we have a need to connect ourselves to valuable others, and to proudly call the resulting collective "we" and "us".

But people do not connect themselves indiscriminately to all other people. When there is a "we", often there also will be a "they" – a group of outsiders that is different from "us". People continuously categorize their social world into ingroups and outgroups, and their own ingroups constitute an important part of their identity. As a consequence, people tend to hold an inflated view of their ingroups and, for instance, perceive their own groups as morally superior – implying that different groups are morally inferior. Feelings of uncertainty and fear increases the human tendency to categorize people into "us" versus "them" and fuels intergroup conflict.[4] Such intergroup conflict can take many forms and may escalate to different degrees, ranging from an uncomfortable atmosphere at a soccer match to bloody wars and genocide. But what most instances of intergroup conflict share is that (1) people connect their own identity more strongly to the ingroup and (2) people perceive the outgroup as threatening.

Conspiracy theories are part and parcel of such perceived intergroup conflict and reflect the mutually suspicious feelings that emerge on both sides of the conflict. Specifically, research finds that conspiracy theories are intimately linked with the two elements of intergroup conflict. First, the more strongly people connect their own identity to the ingroup, the more concerned they are when a fellow ingroup member is harmed – and the more tempting it is to come up with conspiratorial explanations blaming an antagonistic outgroup, particularly if the harm occurred under somewhat mysterious circumstances. Second, the more threatening an outgroup is considered to be – because the outgroup is more powerful, more technologically advanced, carries negative stereotypes, or because the outgroup outnumbers the ingroup – the more likely people are to believe in theories stipulating that members of this outgroup are conspiring against the ingroup. Combined, these insights suggest that conspiracy theories reflect a motivation to protect a valued ingroup from a potentially dangerous outgroup.

Also, the social processes underlying conspiracy theories therefore are not pathological: Conspiracy theories result from the basic human tendency to categorize the world into ingroups and outgroups and from the corresponding desire to protect one's ingroup from powerful outgroups that might be dangerous. The suspicious feelings that people often have about different groups do not have to be irrational and actually can have a protective function: Sometimes outgroups truly can be dangerous or deceptive and plan malevolent actions against one's ingroup. But as we have seen throughout this book, people make many mistakes in this process and frequently see conspiracies where there is unlikely to be one. In sum, there is an intergroup dimension to conspiracy theories: Uncertainty and fear stimulate conspiracy theories, particularly if there is a suspect outgroup to blame for harm experienced by ingroup members.

INSIGHT 3: CONSPIRACY THEORIES ARE ROOTED IN STRONG IDEOLOGIES

People have a moral perspective on the world, and evaluate the behavior of themselves and others as morally "right" or "wrong". These moral judgments are closely related with people's norms and values and form the basis of people's ideological beliefs of what a good society should look like. Ideological beliefs are subjective, however, and people often appreciate that others may hold a different view on how to solve pressing societal issues. This ideological plurality is reflected in the many different political opinions that citizens have, the different political parties in parliament, and intense debates between people about important topics such as climate change, poverty, and public health. But sometimes, people endorse their ideological beliefs with such zeal and conviction that alternative views appear unacceptable. Their ideological beliefs do not seem subjective anymore but appear to dictate an objective, undeniable truth. Such strong ideological beliefs lead people to support extremist political movements or religiously fundamentalist organizations.

Feelings of fear and uncertainty stimulate such rigid, extreme ideological beliefs. To some extent this assertion may seem paradoxical, given that one characteristic of ideological extremism is an excessive conviction in the objective correctness of one's views. But extremism tends to increase as a function of societal circumstances that elicit uncertainty and fear, such as economic recessions, societal turmoil, or the refugee crisis that the EU has seen recently. One psychological theory to explain this paradox is that uncertainty and fear lead to a process termed "compensatory conviction": People compensate for their uncertain feelings in one domain with increased certainty in other domains, most often their ideological beliefs.[5] Such compensatory conviction as an explanation of extreme ideologies is consistent with macro-political insights on extremism. Political scientist Manus Midlarsky extensively studied the rise of extremist regimes around the world in the 20th century and found support for a causal role of the insecurities that citizens experience through what he calls "ephemeral gains".[6] Specifically, the rise of extremism in societies is typically preceded by, first, a short-lived period of prosperity (e.g., in terms of territory or economic growth), followed by a period of critical losses. The societal unrest that these losses generate lead many citizens to embrace extremist political movements that offer simple political solutions to reverse the losses and reinstall the country's previous glory.

As we have seen in Chapter 5, people who endorse extreme ideologies are more likely to believe conspiracy theories than people who endorse moderate ideologies. The evidence for this emerges from both historical sources (i.e., extremist regimes propagate more conspiracy theories than moderate, democratic governments), psychological research (i.e., people who hold extreme ideological beliefs are more likely to believe conspiracy theories than people who hold moderate ideological beliefs), and qualitative research (i.e., underground extremist groups are highly likely to propagate conspiracy theories as part of their core ideology). The relationship between extremism and conspiracy theories is at least partly connected with the previous insight about intergroup conflict: Extreme ideologies have a strong tendency to frame the world into a conflict between "Us" versus "Them" (e.g., "Us" the people versus "Them" the corrupt elites). But there is also more to it than that. Extreme beliefs converge with conspiracy theories in offering clarity about the causes of societal problems. Instead of appreciating the complexity of many developments in society, extremist ideologies assert that societal problems occur for simple reasons – for instance, because they are caused deliberately by corrupt outgroups.

While radical and extremist ideologies have done much harm in the past century, they are not a result of pathology. Extreme ideologies can emerge when people have strong concerns about societal injustices that they perceive and when they endorse their moral beliefs with strong conviction. Furthermore, it should be noted that strong ideological convictions have given humanity not only a lot of bad but also a lot of good. Extremists typically are not stopped by highly agreeable people who are willing to make compromises on everything, including basic human rights. Instead, they are stopped by other extremists, such as activists and organized political movements that draw a firm line in the sand as to what is and is not morally acceptable. Strong ideologies have been responsible for terrorism, oppression, and slavery, but also for important societal change such as increased equality, democracy, and constitutional protection of basic human rights. It was not that long ago when favoring equal rights regardless of race was considered an extremist ideological position (a case in point being the apartheid system in South Africa, which ended in 1991). For better or worse, one aspect of strong ideologies is conspiracy theories, most often about groups holding opposite ideological beliefs.

These three complementary insights offer a straightforward explanation of the prevalence of conspiracy theories. Why are conspiracy theories widespread among normal citizens? Because conspiracy theories are rooted in normal psychological processes that are amplified by negative emotions. Situations that provoke uncertainty and fear overactivate the otherwise functional cognitive processes of pattern perception and agency detection; they also stimulate the human tendency to categorize people into conflicting groups of "us" and "them"; and they intensify people's moral judgments, rendering them more susceptible to extreme ideologies. Furthermore, actual conspiracies can and do occur, making not all conspiracy theories irrational to begin with. It can be functional to be suspicious of powerful outgroups, even when people make a lot of mistakes in the process. Being susceptible to conspiracy theories may be a natural aspect of the human condition.

HOW CAN WE REDUCE CONSPIRACY THEORIES?

Given the observation that real conspiracies sometimes occur, I feel compelled to start a section on reducing conspiracy theories with a clarification: Reducing conspiracy theories is not the same as promoting gullibility among the public. It is also not an attempt to curb efforts to reduce corruption, to suppress dissent among citizens, or to excuse officials who actually commit corruption. Being a good citizen means being a constructively critical citizen who follows the actions of decision makers with great interest, and who speaks his or her mind when seeing bad policy or actual integrity violations. But as I have made clear throughout this book, many conspiracy theories are simply irrational, and often harmful as well. It is irrational and harmful to believe that pharmaceutical companies hide evidence that vaccines cause autism. It is irrational and harmful to believe that climate change is a hoax (perpetrated by the Chinese, corrupt scientists, or others). Members of the public can contribute to good governance with constructive criticism designed to improve policy, but they also can undermine good governance with conspiracy theories that have no basis in reality and ignore the actual problems that society faces. Reducing conspiracy theories does not mean ignoring actual corruption; it means improving people's capacity to recognize when conspiratorial allegations are implausible.

A focus on irrational conspiracy theories would suggest that increasing rationality and offering rational arguments may help in reducing their appeal. This is indeed the case. Analytic thinking reduces the tendency to believe conspiracy theories, and, consistently, efforts to stimulate analytic thinking (e.g., education) are associated with decreased conspiracy beliefs.[7] Furthermore, offering rational arguments can help the public to make an honest evaluation of the plausibility or implausibility of a conspiracy theory. Many conspiracy theories can appear persuasive at first by proffering a set of seemingly rational arguments, sometimes even grounded in scientific claims. An example is the 9/11 "melted steel" theory, which is based on the (scientifically correct) insight that steel does not melt at the temperatures produced by burning kerosene. Hence, so this theory proposes, it follows that it is "scientifically impossible" that the fires that erupted after the crash of the airplanes were the cause of the Twin Towers collapsing. Instead, the towers must have been brought down by a different cause – namely, through controlled demolition.

Arguments such as these can make conspiracy theories appealing to a broad audience: After all, how else should we explain the collapse of the towers if it cannot have been the kerosene fires? In an effort to reduce conspiracy theories, it is important to inform the public of what science actually has to say about these issues. Quite often conspiracy theories appear plausible at first, only to turn implausible if one adds only one crucial piece of extra information. Scientifically, the "melted steel" theory is flawed because it proposes a half-truth: Steel indeed does not melt at the temperatures produced by burning kerosene, but this theory fails to add that steel does not have to melt for the construction to collapse. The steel only needs to weaken up to a certain point for this to happen – and steel weakens enormously at the temperatures produced by burning kerosene, making it impossible to carry the weight of all the floors on top of the construction.

The steel construction of the Twin Towers responded exactly how it would be expected to respond to the plane crashes and the kerosene fires that erupted on that fateful day: It collapsed.

But besides rationality, I suspect that interventions designed to reduce conspiracy theories are particularly likely to be effective when they target the primary cause of conspiracy beliefs: Fear and uncertainty. If one manages to transform widespread pessimism into optimism, irrational conspiracy theories will decrease among the public. As these aversive feelings are closely coupled with feeling out of control, I propose that likewise making people feel in control reduces conspiracy theories. Put differently, people need to experience a sense of *empowerment* in order to become less suspicious: to feel that they can influence their own destiny and that they have a say in the decisions that affect them. Indeed, one study finds that having participants remember a time in their life when they felt completely in control reduced conspiracy theories as compared to a neutral baseline condition.[8]

The insight that empowering people reduces conspiracy theories has implications for what leaders can do to make their followers less suspicious. One basic insight from the leadership literature is that people can govern with different leadership styles, and these styles differ in terms of how much they empower their followers by involving them in decisions. In a study among employees in various organizations that I carried out together with organizational psychologist Reinout de Vries, we examined the question how different leadership styles would predict organizational conspiracy beliefs (that is, employees' beliefs about managers conspiring in secret to pursue evil goals). We specifically looked at four different and frequently occurring leadership styles. These four styles differed in whether they were destructive or constructive.[9]

The destructive leadership styles that we investigated were despotic leadership and laissez-faire leadership. Despotic leadership means being an authoritarian leader who is harsh towards followers and does not easily accept criticism. Laissez-faire leadership essentially means a lack of leadership, as these leaders do not intervene until absolutely necessary. The constructive leadership styles that we investigated were charismatic leadership and participative leadership. Charismatic leaders inspire followers to make the organization's goals their own goals and instill the feeling among employees that their work matters. Participative leaders, in turn, include followers in decision-making processes by asking for their opinions about the decisions to be made that affect them all.

The results indicated that both the destructive leadership styles predicted stronger conspiracy beliefs among employees, which was due to increased feelings of insecurity about their jobs. Despotic leaders made people feel insecure, as these leaders do not appear concerned with the well-being or interests of followers. Likewise, laissez-faire leaders made people feel insecure, as it is difficult for people to get a sense of how much the leader values them if the leader is never around. If the goal is to reduce conspiracy theories, being destructive as a leader – through either active or passive means – is not the answer. Of the more constructive leadership styles, we found that charismatic leadership was unrelated to conspiracy beliefs. Charismatic leadership may influence people in many ways, often positively (e.g., it increases their motivation to exert effort for the collective), but it does not influence the probability that they believe conspiracy theories: People are equally likely to endorse conspiracy theories that involve charismatic or noncharismatic leaders.

There was one leadership style that did predict reduced belief in conspiracy theories, however, and that was the participative leadership style. Leaders who give their followers a voice when important decisions need to be made and who take the input and opinions of followers seriously in their management tasks elicited less conspiracy theories than nonparticipative leaders. The reason is that these leaders empower their followers: Followers feel that they can be part of important decision-making processes and that their opinions matter. In fact, it is not necessary for people to always get their way to experience these empowering effects of participative leadership. If people are included in decision-making process, they also have a better sense of the complexity of the decision to be made and to appreciate that differences in opinion may exist on what the next steps should be. People can accept an unfavorable decision quite well provided that they believe the preceding decision-making procedure was fair. For people to feel empowered they first and foremost need to feel taken seriously and to feel like a respected member of their community. This can be achieved by leaders who make genuine efforts to listen to them and take their interests into account.

The essence of participative leadership is to utilize basic principles of procedural justice in decision making: to make decisions using procedures that followers consider to be fair. The effects of procedural justice on how people respond to decision-making authorities are well documented, and by and large this area of research finds that if people consider procedures to be fair they more easily accept subsequent decisions (even if they disagree with them), experience more positive emotions, feel more respected by authorities, and trust authorities more. Procedural justice thus more generally improves the quality of the relationship between leaders and followers, and this is largely due to people's feelings of empowerment, which are stimulated by authorities who grant them a voice in important decisions, who take them seriously, and who regard them as a full-fledged member of their community. As a consequence, procedural justice may be a powerful tool to reduce conspiracy theories.

Providing people with voice in decision-making processes is only one possible way to improve the perceived fairness of decision-making procedures, but there are also other aspects of procedural justice that I would expect to be conducive in reducing conspiracy theories. Besides voice, procedural justice criteria that seem relevant in particular for conspiracy theories are transparency and accountability. Many conspiracy theories originate from beliefs about what authorities discuss in secret and the ulterior motives that they have to endorse certain policies. Increased transparency and accountability are likely to reduce such suspicious thoughts by providing the public with insights into the difficult dilemmas that authorities often face and the reasons why authorities endorsed a certain course of action over alternative possibilities. In that sense, transparency and accountability also empower the public because they enable people to honestly and critically evaluate policy and to hold leaders accountable for their actions in a more constructive fashion than through conspiracy theories.

To reduce conspiracy theories, one can hence combine interventions that promote rationality with interventions that reduce uncertainty and fear. I would specifically advocate a combination of carefully analyzing widespread conspiracy theories through rational arguments and a full assessment of the available evidence, along with procedural justice interventions that empower people and make them part of important decision-making processes. While these interventions may fail to persuade a relatively small group of people that is strongly invested in the belief that the world is governed by evil conspiracies, they are likely to persuade a much bigger majority that is susceptible to both conspiratorial and nonconspiratorial explanations of impactful societal events.

TO CONCLUDE

Conspiracy theories are not endemic to our modern era – they have occurred throughout human history. People have always experienced uncertainty and fear in response to possible danger, and, as a means of effectively coping with these aversive feelings, people become vigilant to the possible conspiratorial activities of powerful, and possibly hostile, other groups. Such vigilance is not pathological: It is a natural defense mechanism that involves regular psychological processes. Conspiracy theories therefore are common and will continue to be in the foreseeable future. Nevertheless, the fact that some conspiracy theories are common does not make them true or rational. At present the world is facing serious challenges that require responsible solutions but that are also frequent targets of conspiracy theories – including populism, climate change, intergroup conflict, public health, poverty, immigration, unemployment, public governance, and so on. I therefore hope that the insights about the psychology of conspiracy theories that are offered here may contribute to a less paranoid society.

FURTHER READING

Books about conspiracy theories:

- For an interesting popular science book about conspiracy theories, read *Suspicious minds: Why we believe conspiracy theories* by Rob Brotheron (2015; New York, NY: Bloomsbury Sigma).
- For a US political science perspective, read *American conspiracy theories* by Joseph E. Uscinski and Joseph M. Parent (2014; New York, NY: Oxford University Press). This book also contains the study that analyzes more than 100,000 letters over a time period of 120 years, described in Chapter 2.
- For a historical perspective on conspiracy theories, read *Conspiracy: How the paranoid style flourishes and where it comes from* by Daniel Pipes (1997; New York, NY: Simon & Schuster).
- Also of interest is the political-historical approach of *Political paranoia: The psychopolitics of hatred* by Robert S. Robins and Jerrold M. Post (1997; New Haven, CT: Yale University Press).
- For a volume on conspiracy theories in which multiple authors offer their view, read *The psychology of conspiracy* edited by Michal Bilewicz, Aleksandra Cichocka, and Wiktor Soral (2015; Oxon, UK: Routledge).
- For a volume in which various authors address not only conspiracy theories but also the question whether power really does

corrupt, read *Power, politics, and paranoia: Why people are suspicious of their leaders* edited by Jan-Willem van Prooijen and Paul A. M. van Lange (2014; Cambridge, UK: Cambridge University Press).

Books about belief in general:

- For an excellent popular science book about the ideas in Chapter 3 on the architecture of beliefs, read *The believing brain: From ghosts and gods to politics and conspiracies – How we construct beliefs and reinforce them as truths* by Michael Shermer (2011; New York, NY: Henry Holt).
- Another good popular science book on the psychology of belief is "*The belief instinct: The psychology of souls, destiny, and the meaning of life*" by Jesse Bering (2011; New York, NY: W.W. Norton & Co).

Books about populism/extremism and conspiracy theories:

- For a good introduction to populism, read *What is populism?* by Jan-Werner Müller (2016; Philadelphia, PA: University of Pennsylvania Press). The book also addresses the role of conspiracy theories in populist movements.
- For the qualitative study on extremist fringe groups and conspiracy theories, read *The power of unreason: Conspiracy theories, extremism and counter-terrorism* by Jamie Bartlett, J. and Carl Miller (2010; London, UK: Demos).

Books about belief versus reality:

- Do some of the pseudo-scientific "9/11 for truth" conspiracy theories appear plausible to you? Then definitely read *Debunking 9/11 myths: Why conspiracy theories can't stand up to the facts* by David Dunbar and Brad Reagan (2011; New York, NY: Hearst Books). In it, you will learn what scientists and witnesses actually have to say about the conspiracy theories associated with this event.
- Do you feel that there may be a grain of truth in some paranormal phenomena? Please learn about the scientific evidence in *Paranormality: The science of the supernatural* by Richard Wiseman (2011; London, UK: Pan Books).

Other

- Watch how a blacksmith refutes the 9/11 "melted steel" conspiracy theory described in Chapter 6: www.youtube.com/watch?v=FzF1KySHmUA
- See the TV interview in which Prince talks about chemtrails, described in Chapter 1: http://youtu.be/3zEiAQdyAGk
- Read an interview with the author, about the psychology of conspiracy theories: www.vox.com/science-and-health/2017/4/25/15408610/conspiracy-theories-psychologist-explained

NOTES

CHAPTER 1

1 Zonis & Joseph, 1994, p. 448
2 Van Prooijen & Van Lange, 2016
3 Kay, Gaucher, McGregor, & Nash, 2010
4 Wright & Arbuthnot, 1974
5 Pipes, 1997
6 Pipes, 1997
7 Synovate, 2009
8 Oliver & Wood, 2014
9 For details, see Sunstein & Vermeule, 2009

CHAPTER 2

1 Uscinksi & Parent, 2014
2 Andeweg, 2014
3 Pipes, 1997
4 Park, 2010
5 Neuberg, Kenrick, & Schaller, 2011
6 Vuolevi & Van Lange, 2010
7 Van Prooijen & Acker, 2015
8 Sullivan et al., 2010; Van Harreveld et al., 2014; Whitson & Galinsky, 2008

9 Van Prooijen & Acker, 2015
10 Van Prooijen & Jostmann, 2013
11 Leboeuf & Norton, 2012

CHAPTER 3

1 Wiseman, 2015
2 Wood, Douglas, & Sutton, 2012
3 Goertzel, 1994; Swami et al., 2011
4 Darwin, Neave, & Holmes, 2011; Lobato, Mendoza, Sims, & Chin, 2014
5 Aarnio & Lindeman, 2005; Gervais & Norenzayan, 2012; Swami et al., 2014; Van Prooijen, 2017
6 Shermer, 2011
7 Falk & Konold, 1997
8 Wilke, Scheibehenne, Gaissmaier, McCanney, & Barrett, 2014
9 Skinner, 1948
10 Skinner, 1948, p. 171
11 Blackmore & Trościanko, 1985
12 Dieguez, Wagner-Egger, & Gauvrit, 2015
13 Bressan, 2002; Blagrove, French, & Jones, 2006
14 Van Prooijen, Douglas, & De Inocencio, in press
15 Van Elk, 2013
16 Douglas et al., 2016

CHAPTER 4

1 Goertzel, 1994
2 Pipes, 1997
3 Van Prooijen & Van Dijk, 2014
4 Dovidio et al., 2004; Galinsky & Moskowitz, 2000
5 Golec De Zavala & Cichocka, 2012
6 Imhoff & Bruder, 2014
7 Mashuri & Zaduqisti, 2013
8 Mashuri & Zaduqisti, 2015
9 Thorburn & Bogart, 2005
10 Crocker, Luhtanen, Broadnax, & Blaine, 1999

CHAPTER 5

1 www.independent.co.uk/news/uk/politics/eu-referendum-poll-brexit-live-leave-voters-mi5-conspiracy-government-a7092806.html
2 For an overview, see Jost, Glaser, Kruglanski, & Sulloway, 2003.
3 Van Prooijen, Krouwel, Boiten, & Eendebak, 2015; Van Prooijen & Krouwel, 2017
4 Müller, 2016
5 Judis, 2016
6 Pipes, 1997
7 Inglehart, 1987
8 Van Prooijen, Krouwel, & Pollet, 2015
9 Imhoff, 2015
10 Uscinski & Parent, 2014
11 Bartlett & Miller, 2010

CHAPTER 6

1 Whitson & Galinsky, 2008
2 Hogg, Adelman, & Blagg, 2010
3 Eisenberger, Lieberman, & Williams, 2003
4 Hogg, 2007
5 McGregor, 2006
6 Midlarsky, 2011
7 Van Prooijen, 2017
8 Van Prooijen & Acker, 2015
9 Van Prooijen & De Vries, 2016

REFERENCES

Aarnio, K., & Lindeman, M. (2005). Superstition, education and thinking styles. *Personality and Individual Differences*, 39, 1227–1236.

Andeweg, R. B. (2014). A growing confidence gap in politics? Data versus discourse. In J.-W. van Prooijen & P. A. M. van Lange (Eds.), *Power, politics, and paranoia:Why people are suspicious of their leaders* (pp. 176–198). Cambridge, UK: Cambridge University Press.

Bartlett, J., & Miller, C. (2010). *The power of unreason: Conspiracy theories extremism and counter-terrorism*. London, UK: Demos.

Blackmore, S., & Trościanko, T. (1985). Belief in the paranormal: Probability judgements, illusory control, and the 'chance baseline shift'. *British Journal of Psychology*, 76, 459–468.

Blagrove, M., French, C., & Jones, G. (2006). Probabilistic reasoning, affirmative bias and belief in precognitive dreams. *Applied Cognitive Psychology*, 20, 65–83.

Bressan, P. (2002).The connection between random sequences, everyday coincidences, and belief in the paranormal. *Applied Cognitive Psychology*, 16, 17–34.

Cowburn, A. (2016, June 21). EU referendum: Poll reveals third of Leave voters believe MI5 conspiring with government to stop Brexit. *Independent*.

Crocker, J., Luhtanen, R., Broadnax, S., & Blaine, B. E. (1999). Belief in U.S. government conspiracies against Blacks among Black and White college students: Powerlessness or system blame? *Personality and Social Psychology Bulletin*, 25, 941–953.

Darwin, H., Neave, N., & Holmes, J. (2011). Belief in conspiracy theories: The role of paranormal belief, paranoid ideation and schizotypy. *Personality and Individual Differences, 50,* 1289–1293.

Dieguez, S., Wagner-Egger, P., & Gauvrit, N. (2015). Nothing happens by accident, or does it? A low prior for randomness does not explain belief in conspiracy theories. *Psychological Science, 26,* 1762–1770.

Douglas, K. M., Sutton, R. M., Callan, M. J., Dawtry, R. J., & Harvey, A. J. (2016). Someone is pulling the strings: Hypersensitive agency detection and belief in conspiracy theories. *Thinking and Reasoning, 22,* 57–77.

Dovidio, J. F., ten Vergert, M., Steward, T. L., Gaertner, S. L., Johnson, J. D., Esses, V. M., Riek, B. M., & Pearson, A. R. (2004). Perspective and prejudice: Antecedents and mediating mechanisms. *Personality and Social Psychology Bulletin, 30,* 1537–1549.

Eisenberger, N. I., Lieberman, M. D., & Williams, K. D. (2003). Does rejection hurt? A fMRI study of social exclusion. *Science, 302,* 290–292.

Falk, R., & Konold, C. (1997). Making sense of randomness: Implicit encoding as a basis for judgment. *Psychological Review, 104,* 301–318.

Galinsky, A. D., & Moskowitz, G. B. (2000). Perspective-taking: Decreasing stereotype expression, stereotype accessibility, and in-group favoritism. *Journal of Personality and Social Psychology, 78,* 708–724.

Gervais, W. M., & Norenzayan, A. (2012). Analytic thinking promotes religious disbelief. *Science, 336,* 493–496.

Goertzel, T. (1994). Belief in conspiracy theories. *Political Psychology, 15,* 733–744.

Golec de Zavala, A., & Cichocka, A. (2012). Collective narcissism and anti-Semitism in Poland. *Group Processes and Intergroup Relations, 15,* 213–229.

Hogg, M. A. (2007). Uncertainty-identity theory. *Advances in Experimental Social Psychology, 39,* 69–126.

Hogg, M. A., Adelman, J. R., & Blagg, R. D. (2010). Religion in the face of uncertainty: An uncertainty-identity theory account of religiousness. *Personality and Social Psychology Review, 14,* 72–83.

Imhoff, R. (2015). Beyond (right-wing) authoritarianism: Conspiracy mentality as an incremental predictor of prejudice. In M. Bilewicz, A. Cichocka, & W. Soral (Eds.), *The Psychology of Conspiracy* (pp. 122–141). Oxon, UK: Routledge.

Imhoff, R., & Bruder, M. (2014). Speaking (un-)truth to power: Conspiracy mentality as a generalized political attitude. *European Journal of Personality, 28,* 25–43.

Inglehart, R. (1987). Extremist political position and perceptions of conspiracy: Even paranoids have real enemies. In C. F. Graumann & S. Moscovici (Eds.), *Changing conceptions of conspiracy* (pp. 231–244). New York, NY: Springer-Verlag.

Jost, J. J., Glaser, J., Kruglanski, A. W., & Sulloway, F. J. (2003). Political conservatism as motivated social cognition. *Psychological Bulletin, 129*, 339–375.

Judis, J. B. (2016). *The populist explosion: How the great recession transformed American and European politics.* New York, NY: Columbia Global Reports.

Kay, A. C., Gaucher, D., McGregor, I., & Nash, K. (2010). Religious conviction as compensatory control. *Personality and Social Psychology Review, 14*, 37–48.

LeBoeuf, R. A., & Norton, M. I. (2012). Consequence-cause matching: Looking to the consequences of events to infer their causes. *Journal of Consumer Research, 39*, 128–141.

Lobato, E., Mendoza, J., Sims, V., & Chin, M. (2014). Examining the relationship between conspiracy theories, paranormal beliefs, and pseudoscience acceptance among a university population. *Applied Cognitive Psychology, 28*, 617–625.

Mashuri, A., & Zaduqisti, E. (2013). The role of social identification, intergroup threat, and out-group derogation in explaining belief in conspiracy theory about terrorism in Indonesia. *International Journal of Research Studies in Psychology, 3*, 35–50.

Mashuri, A., & Zaduqisti, E. (2015). The effect of intergroup threat and social identity salience on the belief in conspiracy theories over terrorism in Indonesia: Collective angst as a mediator. *International Journal of Psychological Research, 8*, 24–35.

McGregor, I. (2006). Offensive defensiveness: Toward an integrative neuroscience of compensatory zeal after mortality salience, personal uncertainty, and other poignant self-threats. *Psychological Inquiry, 17*, 299–308.

Midlarsky, M. L. (2011). *Origins of political extremism.* Cambridge, UK: Cambridge University Press.

Müller, J.-W. (2016). *What is populism?* Philadelphia, PA: University of Pennsylvania Press.

Neuberg, S. L., Kenrick, D. T., & Schaller, M. (2011). Human threat management systems: Self-protection and disease avoidance. *Neuroscience and Biobehavioral Reviews, 35*, 1042–1051.

Oliver, J. E., & Wood, T. (2014). Medical conspiracy theories and health behaviors in the United States. *JAMA Internal Medicine, 174*, 817–818.

Park, C. L. (2010). Making sense of the meaning literature: An integrative review of meaning making and its effects on adjustment to stressful life events. *Psychological Bulletin, 136,* 257–301.

Pipes, D. (1997). *Conspiracy: How the paranoid style flourishes and where it comes from.* New York, NY: Simon & Schuster.

Shermer, M. (2011). *The believing brain: From ghosts and gods to politics and conspiracies – How we construct beliefs and reinforce them as truths.* New York, NY: Henry Holt.

Skinner, B. F. (1948). 'Superstition' in the pigeon. *Journal of Experimental Psychology, 38,* 168–172.

Sullivan, D., Landau, M. J., & Rothschild, Z. K. (2010). An existential function of enemyship: Evidence that people attribute influence to personal and political enemies to compensate for threats to control. *Journal of Personality and Social Psychology, 98,* 434–449.

Sunstein, C. R., & Vermeule, A. (2009). Conspiracy theories: Causes and cures. *The Journal of Political Philosophy, 17,* 202–227.

Swami, V., Coles, R., Stieger, S., Pietschnig, J., Furnham, A., Rehim, S., & Voracek, M. (2011). Conspiracist ideation in Britain and Austria: Evidence of a monological belief system and associations between individual psychological differences and real-world and fictitious conspiracy theories. *British Journal of Psychology, 102,* 443–463.

Swami, V., Voracek, M., Stieger, S., Tran, U. S., & Furnham, A. (2014). Analytic thinking reduces belief in conspiracy theories. *Cognition, 133,* 572–585.

Synovate (2009). *Geloven Nederlanders in Complottheorieen?* Research report Synovate, 13 May 2009.

Thorburn, S., & Bogart, L. M. (2005). Conspiracy beliefs about birth control: Barriers to pregnancy prevention among African-Americans of reproductive age. *Health Education & Behavior, 32,* 474–487.

Uscinski, J. E., & Parent, J. M. (2014). *American conspiracy theories.* New York, NY: Oxford University Press.

Van Elk, M. (2013). Paranormal believers are more prone to illusory agency detection than skeptics. *Consciousness and Cognition, 22,* 1041–1046.

Van Harreveld, F., Rutjens, B. T., Schneider, I. K., Nohlen, H. U., & Keskinis, K. (2014). In doubt and disorderly: Ambivalence promotes compensatory perceptions of order. *Journal of Experimental Psychology: General, 143,* 1666–1676.

Van Prooijen, J.-W. (2017). Why education predicts decreased belief in conspiracy theories. *Applied Cognitive Psychology, 31,* 50–58.

Van Prooijen, J.-W., & Acker, M. (2015). The influence of control on belief in conspiracy theories: Conceptual and applied extensions. *Applied Cognitive Psychology*, 29, 753–761.

Van Prooijen, J.-W., & De Vries, R. E. (2016). Organizational conspiracy beliefs: Implications for leadership styles and employee outcomes. *Journal of Business and Psychology*, 31, 479–491.

Van Prooijen, J.-W., Douglas, K., & De Inocencio, C. (in press). Connecting the dots: Illusory pattern perception predicts belief in conspiracies and the supernatural. *European Journal of Social Psychology.*

Van Prooijen, J.-W., & Jostmann, N. B. (2013). Belief in conspiracy theories: The influence of uncertainty and perceived morality. *European Journal of Social Psychology*, 43, 109–115.

Van Prooijen, J.-W., & Krouwel, A. P. M. (2017). Extreme political beliefs predict dogmatic intolerance. *Social Psychological and Personality Science*, 8, 292–300.

Van Prooijen, J.-W., Krouwel, A. P. M., Boiten, M., & Eendebak, L. (2015). Fear among the extremes: How political ideology predicts negative emotions and outgroup derogation. *Personality and Social Psychology Bulletin*, 41, 485–497.

Van Prooijen, J.-W., Krouwel, A. P. M., & Pollet, T. (2015). Political extremism predicts belief in conspiracy theories. *Social Psychological and Personality Science*, 6, 570–578.

Van Prooijen, J.-W., & Van Dijk, E. (2014). When consequence size predicts belief in conspiracy theories: The moderating role of perspective taking. *Journal of Experimental Social Psychology*, 55, 63–73.

Van Prooijen, J.-W., & Van Lange, P. A. M. (2016). *Cheating, corruption, and concealment: The roots of dishonesty.* Cambridge, UK: Cambridge University Press.

Vuolevi, J. H. K., & Van Lange, P. A. M. (2010). Beyond the information given: The power of a belief in self-interest. *European Journal of Social Psychology*, 40, 26–34.

Whitson, J. A., & Galinsky, A. D. (2008). Lacking control increases illusory pattern perception. *Science*, 322, 115–117.

Wilke, A., Scheibehenne, B., Gaissmaier, W., McCanney, P., & Barrett, H. C. (2014). Illusory pattern detection in habitual gamblers. *Evolution and Human Behavior*, 35, 291–297.

Wiseman, R. (2015). *Paranormality: The science of the supernatural.* London, UK: Pan Books.

Wood, M. J., Douglas, K. M., & Sutton, R. M. (2012). Dead and alive: Beliefs in contradictory conspiracy theories. *Social Psychological and Personality Science*, 3, 767–773.

Wright, T. L., & Arbuthnot, J. (1974). Interpersonal trust, political preference, and perceptions of the Watergate affair. *Personality and Social Psychology Bulletin*, 1, 168–170.

Zonis, M., & Joseph, C. M. (1994). Conspiracy thinking in the middle east. *Political Psychology*, 15, 443–459.

Printed in the United States
by Baker & Taylor Publisher Services